Dragons of the Air

by H. G. Seeley

PREFACE

I was a student of law at a time when Sir Richard Owen was lecturing on Extinct Fossil Reptiles. The skill of the great master, who built bones together as a child builds with a box of bricks, taught me that the laws which determine the forms of animals were less understood at that time than the laws which govern the relations of men in their country. The laws of Nature promised a better return of new knowledge for reasonable study. A lecture on Flying Reptiles determined me to attempt to fathom the mysteries which gave new types of life to the Earth and afterwards took them away.

Thus I became the very humble servant of the Dragons of the Air. Knowing but little about them I went to Cambridge, and for ten years worked with the Professor of Geology, the late Rev. Adam Sedgwick, LL.D., F.R.S., in gathering their bones from the so-called Cambridge Coprolite bed, the Cambridge Greensand. The bones came in thousands, battered and broken, but instructive as better materials might not have been. My rooms became filled with remains of existing birds, lizards, and mammals, which threw light on the astonishing collection of old bones which I assisted in bringing together for the University.

In time I had something to say about Flying Animals which was new. The story was told in the theatre of the Royal Institution, in a series of lectures. Some of them were repeated in several English towns. There was still much to learn of foreign forms of flying animals; but at last, with the aid of the Government grant administered by the Royal Society, and the chiefs of the great Continental museums, I saw all the specimens in Europe.

So I have again written out my lectures, with the aid of the latest discoveries, and the story of animal structure has lost nothing in interest as a twice-told tale. It still presents in epitome the story of life on the Earth. He who understands whence the Flying Reptiles came, how they endured, and disappeared from the Earth, has solved some of the greatest mysteries of life. I have only contributed something towards solving the problems.

In telling my story, chiefly of facts in Nature, an attempt is made to show how a naturalist does his work, in the hope that perhaps a few readers will find happiness in following the workings of the laws of life. Such an illumination has proved to many worth seeking, a solid return for labour, which is not to be marketed on the Exchange, but may be taken freely without exhausting the treasury of Nature's truths. Such outlines of knowledge as here are offered to a larger public, may also, I believe, be acceptable to students of science and scientific men.

The drawings given in illustration of the text have been made for me by Miss E. B. Seeley.

H. G. S. KENSINGTON, May, 1901

CONTENTS

DRAGONS OF THE AIR

CHAPTER I

FLYING REPTILES

The history of life on the earth during the epochs of geological time unfolds no more wonderful discovery among types of animals which have become extinct than the family of fossils known as flying reptiles. Its coming into existence, its structure, and passing away from the living world are among the great mysteries of Nature.

The animals are astonishing in their plan of construction. In aspect they are unlike birds and beasts which, in this age, hover over land and sea. They gather into themselves in the body of a single individual, structures which, at the present day, are among the most distinctive characters of certain mammals, birds, and reptiles.

The name "flying reptile" expresses this anomaly. Its invention is due to the genius of the great French naturalist Cuvier, who was the first to realise that this extinct animal, entombed in slabs of stone, is one of the wonders of the world.

The word "reptile" has impressed the imagination with unpleasant sound, even when the habits of the animals it indicates are unknown. It is familiarly associated with life which is reputed venomous, and is creeping and cold. Its common type, the serpent, in many parts of the world takes a yearly toll of victims from man and beast, and has become the representative of silent, active strength, dreaded craft, and danger.

Science uses the word "reptile" in a more exact way, to define the assemblage of cold-blooded animals which in familiar description are separately named serpents, lizards, turtles, hatteria, and crocodiles.

Turtles and the rest of them survive from great geological antiquity. They present from age to age diversity of aspect and habit, and in unexpected differences of outward proportion of the body show how the laws of life have preserved each animal type. For the vital organs which constitute each animal a reptile, and the distinctive bony structures with which they are associated, remain unaffected, or but little modified, by the animal's external change in appearance.

The creeping reptile is commonly imagined as the antithesis of the bird. For the bird overcomes the forces that hold even man to the earth, and enjoys exalted aerial conditions of life. Therefore the marvel is shared equally by learned and unlearned, that the power of flight should have been an endowment of animals sprung from the breed of serpents, or crocodiles, enabling them to move through the air as though they too were of a heaven-born race. The wonder would not be lessened if the animal were a degraded representative of a nobler type, or if it should be demonstrated that even beasts have advanced in the battle of life. The winged reptile, when compared with a bird, is not less astounding than the poetic conceptions in Milton's Paradise Lost of degradation which overtakes life that once was amongst the highest. And on the other hand, from the point of view of the teaching of Darwin in the theories of modern science, we are led to ask whether a flying reptile may not be evidence of the physical exaltation which raises animals in the scale of organisation. The dominance upon the earth of flying reptiles during the great middle period of geological history will long engage the interest of those who can realise the complexity of its structure, or care to unravel the meaning of the procession of animal forms in successive geological ages which preceded the coming of man.

The outer vesture of an animal counts for little in estimating the value of ties which bind orders of animals together, which are included in the larger classes of life. The kindred relationship which makes the snake of the same class as the tortoise is determined by the soft vital organs--brain, heart, lungs--which are the essentials of an animal's existence and control its way of life. The wonder which science weaves into the meaning of the word "reptile," "bird," or "mammal," is partly in exhibiting minor changes of character in those organs and other soft parts, but far more in showing that while they endure unchanged, the hard parts of the skeleton are modified in many ways. For the bones of the reptile orders stretch their affinities in one direction towards the skeletons of salamanders and fishes; and extend them also at the same time in other directions, towards birds and mammals. This mystery we may hope to partly unravel.

CHAPTER II

HOW A REPTILE IS KNOWN

DEFINITION OF REPTILES BY THEIR VITAL ORGANS

The relations of reptiles to other animals may be stated so as to make evident the characters and affinities which bind them together. Early in the nineteenth century naturalists included with the Reptilia the tribe of salamanders and frogs which are named Amphibia. The two groups have been separated from each other because the young of Amphibia pass through a tadpole stage of development. They then breathe by gills, like fishes, taking oxygen from the air which is suspended in water, before lungs are acquired which afterwards enable the animals to take oxygen directly from the air. The amphibian sometimes sheds the gills, and leaves the water to live on land. Sometimes gills and lungs are retained through life in the same individual. This amphibian condition of lung and gill being present at the same time is paralleled by a few fishes which still exist, like the Australian Ceratodus, the lung-fish, an ancient type of fish which belongs to early days in geological time.

This metamorphosis has been held to separate the amphibian type from the reptile because no existing reptile develops gills or undergoes a metamorphosis. Yet the character may not be more important as a ground for classification than the community of gills and lungs in the fish and amphibian is ground for putting them together in one natural group. For although no gills are found in reptiles, birds, or mammals, the embryo of each in an early stage of development appears to possess gill-arches, and gill-clefts between them, through which gills might have been developed, even in the higher vertebrates, if the conditions of life had been favourable to such modification of structure. In their bones Reptiles and Amphibia have much in common. Nearly all true reptiles lay eggs, which are defined like those of birds by comparatively large size, and are contained in shells. This condition is not usual in amphibians or fishes. When hatched the young reptile is completely formed, the image of its parent, and has no need to grow a covering to its skin like some birds, or shed its tail like some tadpoles. The reptile is like the bird in freedom from important changes of form after the egg is hatched; and the only structure shed by both is the little horn upon the nose, with which the embryo breaks the shell and emerges a reptile or a bird, growing to maturity with small subsequent variations in the proportions of the body.

THE REPTILE SKIN

Between one class of animals and another the differences in the condition of the skin are more or less distinctive. In a few amphibians there are some bones in the skin on the under side of the body, though the skin is usually naked, and in frogs is said to transmit air to the blood, so as to exercise a respiratory function of a minor kind. This naked condition, so unlike the armoured skin of the true Reptilia, appears to have been paralleled by a number of extinct groups of fossils of the Secondary rocks, such as Ichthyosaurs and Plesiosaurs, which were aquatic, and probably also by some Dinosauria, which were terrestrial.

Living reptiles are usually defended with some kind of protection to the skin. Among snakes and lizards the skin has commonly a covering of overlapping scales, usually of horny or bony texture. The tortoise and turtle tribe shut up the animal in a true box of bone, which is cased with an armour of horny plates. Crocodiles have a thick skin embedding a less continuous coat of mail. Thus the skin of a reptile does not at first suggest anything which might become an organ of flight; and its dermal appendages, or scales, may seem further removed from the feathers which ensure flying powers to the bird than from the naked skin of a frog.

THE REPTILE BRAIN

Although the mode of development of the young and the covering of the skin are conspicuous among important characters by which animals are classified, the brain is an organ of some importance, although of greater weight in the higher Vertebrata than in its lower groups. Reptiles have links in the mode of arrangement of the parts of their brains with fishes and amphibians. The regions of that organ are commonly arranged in pairs of nervous masses, known as (1) the olfactory lobes, (2) the cerebrum, behind which is the minute pineal body, followed by (3) the pair of optic lobes, and hindermost of all (4) the single mass termed the cerebellum. These parts of the brain are extended in longitudinal order, one behind the other in all three groups. The olfactory lobes of the brain in Fishes may be as large as the cerebrum; but among Reptiles and Amphibians they are relatively smaller, and they assume more of the condition found in mammals like the Hare or Mole, being altogether subordinate in size. And the cerebral masses begin to be wider and higher than the other parts of the brain, though they do not extend forward above the olfactory lobes, as is often seen in Mammals. In Crocodiles the cerebral hemispheres have a tendency to a broad circular form. Among Chelonian reptiles that region of the brain is more remarkable for height. Lizards and Ophidians both have this part of the brain somewhat pear-shaped, pointed in front, and elongated. The amphibian brain only differs from the lizard type in degree; and differences between lizards' and amphibian brains are less noticeable than between the other orders of reptiles. The reptilian brain is easily distinguished from that of all other animals by the position and proportions of its regions (see Fig. 19, p. 53).

Birds have the parts of the brain formed and arranged in a way that is equally distinctive. The cerebral lobes are relatively large and convex, and deserve the descriptive name "hemispheres." They are always smooth, as among the lower Mammals, and extend backward so as to abut against the hind brain, termed the cerebellum. This junction is brought about in a peculiar way. The cerebral hemispheres in a bird do not extend backward to override the optic lobes, and hide them, as occurs among adult mammals, but they extend back between the optic lobes, so as to force them apart and push them aside, downward and backward, till they extend laterally beyond the junction of the cerebrum with the cerebellum. The brain of a Bird is never reptilian; but in the young Mammal the brain has a very reptilian aspect, because both have their parts primarily arranged in a line. Therefore the brain appears to determine the boundary between bird and reptile exactly.

REPTILIAN BREATHING ORGANS

The breathing organs of Birds and Reptiles which are associated with these different types of brain are not quite the same. The Frog has a cellular lung which, in the details of the minute sacs which branch and cluster at the terminations of the tubes, is not unlike the condition in a Mammal. In a mammal respiration is aided by the bellows-like action of the muscles connected with the ribs, which encase the cavity where the lungs are placed, and this structure is absent in the Frog and its allies. The Frog, on the other hand, has to swallow air in much the same way as man swallows water. The air is similarly grasped by the muscles, and conveyed by them downward to the lungs. Therefore a Frog keeps its mouth shut, and the animal dies from want of air if its mouth is open for a few minutes.

Crocodiles commonly lie in the sun with their mouths widely open. The lungs in both Crocodiles and Turtles are moderately dense, traversed by great bronchial tubes, but do not differ essentially in plan from those of a Frog, though the great branches of the bronchial tubes are stronger, and the air chambers into which the lung is divided are somewhat smaller. The New Zealand Hatteria has the lungs of this cellular type, though rather resembling the amphibian than the Crocodile. The lungs during life in all these animals attain considerable size, the maximum dimensions being found in the terrestrial tortoises, which owe much of their elevated bulk to the dimensions of the air cells which form the lungs.

The lungs of Serpents and Lizards are formed on a different plan. In both those groups of reptiles the dense cellular tissue is limited to the part of the lung which is nearest to the throat. This network of blood vessels and air cells extends about the principal bronchial tube much as in other animals, but as it extends backward the blood vessels become few until the tubular lung appears in its hinder part, as it extends down the body, almost as simple in structure as the air bladder of a fish. Among Serpents only one of these tubular lungs is commonly present, and the structure has a less efficient appearance as a breathing organ than the single lung of the fish Ceratodus (Fig. 1). The Chameleons are a group of lizards which differ in many ways from most of their nearest kindred, and the lungs, while conforming in general plan to the lizard type in being dense at the throat, and a tubular bladder in the body, give off on both sides a number of short lateral branches like the fingers of a glove (Fig. 18, p. 51).

Thus the breathing organs of reptiles present two or three distinct types which have caused Serpents and Lizards to be associated in one group by most naturalists who have studied their anatomy; while Crocodiles and Chelonians represent a type of lung which is quite different, and in those groups has much in common. These characters of the breathing organs contribute to separate the cold-blooded armoured reptiles from the warm-blooded birds clothed with feathers, as well as from the warm-blooded mammals which suckle their young; for both these higher groups have denser and more elastic spongy lung tissue.

It will be seen hereafter that many birds in the most active development of their breathing organs substantially revert to the condition of the Serpent or Chameleon in a somewhat modified way. Because, instead of having one great bronchial tube expanded to form a vast reservoir of air which can be discharged from the lung in which the reptile has accumulated it, the bird has the lateral branches of the bronchial tubes prolonged so as to pierce the walls of the lung, when its covering membrane expands to form many air cells, which fill much of the cavity of the bird's body (see Fig. 16). Thus the bird appears to combine the characters of such a lung as that of a Crocodile, with a condition which has some analogy with the lung of a Chameleon. It is this link of structure of the breathing organs between reptiles and birds that constitutes one of the chief interests of flying reptiles, for they prove to have possessed air cells prolonged from the lungs, which extended into the bones.

CHAPTER III

A REPTILE IS KNOWN BY ITS BONES

Such are a few illustrations of ways in which reptiles resemble other animals, and differ from them, in the organs by means of which the classification of animals is made. But such an idea is incomplete without noticing that the bony framework of the body associated with such vital organs also shows in its chief parts that reptiles are easily recognised by their bones. I will therefore briefly state how reptiles are defined in some regions of the skeleton, for in tracing the history of reptile life the bones are the principal remains of animals preserved in the rocks; and the soft organs which have perished can only be inferred to have been present from the persistence of durable characteristic parts of the skeleton, which are associated with those soft organs in animals which exist at the present day, and are unknown in other animals in which the skeleton is different.

THE HANG OF THE LOWER JAW

The manner in which the lower jaw is connected with the skull yields one of the most easily recognised differences between the great groups of vertebrate animals.

In Mammals.--In every mammal--such as the Dog or Sheep--the lower jaw, which is formed of one bone on each side, joins directly on to the head of the animal, and moves upon a bone of the skull which is named the temporal bone. This character is sufficient to prove, by the law of association of soft and hard parts of the body, that such an animal had warm blood and suckled its young.

Comparison to show the articulation with the lower jaw in a mammal and Pterodactylus Kochi. The quadrate bone is lettered Q in this Pterodactyle, and comes between the skull and the lower jaw like the quadrate bone in a bird and in lizards.]

In Birds.--In birds a great difference is found in this region of the head. The temporal bone, which it will be more convenient to name the squamosal bone, from its squamous or scale-like form, is still a part of the brain case, and assists in covering the brain itself, exactly as among mammals. But the lower jaw is now made up of five or six bones. And between the hindermost and the squamosal there is an intervening bar of bone, unknown among mammalia, which moves upon the skull by a joint, just as the lower jaw moves upon it. This movable bone unites with parts of the palate and the face, and is known as the quadrate bone. Its presence proves that the animal possessing it laid eggs, and if the face bones join its outer border just above the lower jaw, it proves that the animal possessed hot blood.

In Reptiles.--All reptiles are also regarded as possessing the quadrate bone. But the squamosal bone with which it always unites is in less close union with the brain case, and never covers the brain itself. Serpents show an extreme divergence in this condition from birds, for the squamosal bone appears to be a loose external plate of bone which rests upon the compact brain case and gives attachment to the quadrate bone which is as free as in a bird. Among Lizards the quadrate bone is usually almost as free. In the other division of existing Reptilia, including Crocodiles, the New Zealand lizard-like reptile Hatteria, called Tuatera, and Turtles, the squamosal and quadrate bones are firmly united with the bones of the brain case, face, and palate, so that the quadrate bone has no movement; and the same condition appears in amphibians, such as Toads and Frogs. With these conditions of the quadrate bone are associated cold blood, terrestrial life, and young developed from eggs.

In Fishes.--Bony fishes, and all others in which separate bones build up the skull, differ from Reptiles and Birds much as those animals differ from Mammals. The union of the lower jaw with the skull becomes complicated by the presence of additional bones. The quadrate bone still forms a pulley articulation upon which the lower jaw works, but between it and the squamosal bone is the characteristic bone of the fish known as the hyomandibular, commonly connected with opercular bones and metapterygoid which intervene, and help to unite the quadrate with the brain case. In the Cartilaginous fishes there is only one bone connecting the jaws with the skull on each side. This appears to prove that just as the structure of the arch of bones suspending the jaw may be complicated by the mysterious process called segmentation, which separates a bone into portions, so simplification and variation may result because the primitive divisions of the material cease to be made which exists before bones are formed.

The principal regions of the skull and skeleton all vary in the chief groups of animals with backbones; so that the Reptile may be recognised among fossils, even in extinct groups of animals and occasionally restored from a fragment, to the aspect which characterised it while it lived.

CHAPTER IV

ANIMALS WHICH FLY

The nature of a reptile is now sufficiently intelligible for something to be said concerning flight, and structures by means of which some animals lift themselves in the air. It is not without interest to remember that, from the earliest periods in human records, representations have been made of animals which were furnished with wings, yet walked upon four feet, and in their typical aspect have the head shaped like that of a bird. They are commonly named Dragons.

FLYING DRAGONS

The effigy of the dragon survives to the present day in the figure over which St. George triumphs, on the reverse of the British sovereign. In the luxuriant imaginations of ancient Eastern peoples, dating back to prehistoric ages, perhaps 5000 B.C., the dragons present an astonishing constancy of form. In after-times they underwent a curious evolution, as the conception of Babylon and Egypt is traced through Assyria to Greece. The Wings, which had been associated at first with the fore limb of the typical dragon, become characteristic of the Lion, and of the poet's winged Horse, and finally of the Human figure itself, carved on the great columns of the Greek temples of Ephesus. These flying animals are historically descendants of the same common stock with the dragons of China and Japan, which still preserve the aspect of reptiles. Their interest is chiefly in evidence of a latent spirit of evolution in days too remote for its meaning to be now understood, which has carried the winged forms higher and ever higher in grade of organisation, till their wings ceased to be associated with feelings of terror. The Hebrew cherubim are regarded by H. E. Ryle, Bishop of Exeter, as probably Dragons, and the figure of the conventional angel is the human form of the Dragon.

ORGANS OF FLIGHT

Turning from this reference to the realm of mythology to existing nature, the power of flight is popularly associated with all the chief types of vertebrate animals--fishes, frogs, lizards, birds, and mammals. Many of the animals ill deserve the name of flyers, and most are exceptions to different conditions of existence which control their kindred, but it is convenient to examine for a little the nature of the structures by which this movement in the air, which is not always flight, is made possible. Certain fishes, like the lung-fish Ceratodus, of Queensland, and the mud-fish Lepidosiren, are capable of leaving the water and living on land, and for a time breathe air. But neither these fishes nor Periophthalmus, which runs with rapid movement of its fins and carries the body more or less out of water, or the climbing perch, Anabas, carried out of water over the country by Indian jugglers, ever put on the slightest approach to wings.

FLYING FISHES

The flight of fishes is a kind of parachute support not unlike that by which a folded paper is made to travel in the air. It is chiefly seen in the numerous species of a genus Exocoetus, allied to the gar-pike (Belone), which is common in tropical seas, and usually from a foot to eighteen inches long. They emerge from the water, and for a time support themselves in the air by means of the greatly developed breast fins, which sometimes extend backward to the tail fin. Although these fins appear to correspond to the fore limbs of other animals, they may not be moved at the will of the fish like the wing of a bird. When the flying fishes are seen in shoals in the vicinity of ships, those fins remain extended, so that the fish is said sometimes to travel 200 yards at a speed of fifteen miles an hour, rising twenty feet or more above the surface of the sea, travelling in a straight line, though sometimes influenced by the wind. Here the organ, which is at once a fin and a wing, consists of a number of thin long rods, or rays, which are connected by membrane, and vary in length to form an outline not unlike the wing of a bird which tapers to a point. The interest of these animals is chiefly in the fact that flight is separated from the condition of having lungs with which it is associated in birds, for although the flying fish has an air bladder, there is no duct to connect it with the throat.

FLYING FROGS

The membranes of the foot and hand extend between the metatarsal and metacarpal bones, as well as the bones of the digits.]

Among amphibians the organs of flight are also of a parachute kind, but of a different nature. They are seen in certain frogs which frequent trees, and are limited to membranes which extend between the diverging digits of the hand and foot, forming webs as fully developed as in the foot of a swimming bird. As these frogs leap, the membranes are expanded and help to support the weight of the body, so that the animal descends more easily as it moves from branch to branch. There is no evidence that the bones of the digits ever became elongated like the fin rays of the flying fish or the wing bones of a Bat; but the web suggests the basis of such a wing, and the possibilities under which wings may first originate, by elongation of the bones of a webbed hand like that of a Flying Frog.

FLYING LIZARDS

The Reptilia in their several orders are remarkable for absence of any modification of the arms which might suggest a capacity for acquiring wings, as being latent in their organisation. Crocodiles, Tortoises, and Serpents are alike of the earth, and not of the air. But among Lizards there are small groups of animals in which a limited capacity for movement through the air is developed. It is best known in the family of small lizards named Dragons, represented typically by the species Draco volans found in the Oriental region of the East Indies and Malay Archipelago.

The organ of flight is produced in an unexpected way, by means of the ribs instead of the limbs. The ribs extend outward as far as the arms can stretch, and the first five or six are prolonged beyond the body so as to spread a fold of skin on each side between the arm and the leg. The membrane admits of some movement with the ribs. This arrangement forms a parachute, which enables the animal to move rapidly among branches of trees, extending the structure at will, so that it is used with rapidity too quick to be followed by the eye, as it leaps through considerable distances.

A less singular aid to movement in the air is found in some of the lizards termed Geckos. The so-called Flying Gecko (Platydactylus homalocephalus) has a fringe unconnected with ribs, which extends laterally on the sides of the body and tail, as well as at the back and front of the fore and hind limbs, and between the digits, where the web is sometimes almost as well developed as among Tree Frogs. This is essentially a lateral horizontal frill, extending round the body. Its chief interest is in the circumstance that it includes a membrane which extends between the wrist bones and the shoulder on the front of the arm. That is the only part of the fringe which represents the wing membrane of a bird. The fossil flying reptiles have not only that membrane, but the lateral membranes at the sides of the body and behind the arms.

Other lizards have the skin developed in the direction of the circumference of the body. In the Australian Chlamydosaurus it forms an immense frill round the neck like a mediaeval collar. But though such an adornment might break a fall, it could not be regarded as an organ of flight.

FLYING BIRDS

The wings of birds, when they are developed so as to minister to flight, are all made upon one plan; but as examples of the variation which the organs contributing to make the fore limb manifest, I may instance the short swimming limb of the Penguin, the practically useless rudiment of a wing found in the Ostrich or Kiwi, and the fully developed wing of the Pigeon. The wings of birds obtain an extensive surface to support the animal by muscular movements of three modifications of structure. First, the bones of the fore limb are so shaped that they cannot, in existing birds, be applied to the ground for support and be used like the limbs of quadrupeds, and are therefore folded up at the sides of the body, and carried in an unused or useless state so long as the animal hops on the ground or walks, balancing its weight on the hind legs. Secondly, there are two small folds of skin, less conspicuous than those on the arms of Geckos; one is between the wrist bones and the shoulder, and the smaller hinder membrane is between the upper arm and the body. These membranous expansions are insignificant, and would in themselves be inadequate to support the body or materially assist its movements. Thirdly, the bird develops appendages to the skin which are familiarly known as feathers, and the large feathers which make the wing are attached to the skin covering the lower arm bone named the ulna, and the other bones which represent the wrist and hand. The area and form of the bird's wing are due to individual appendages to the skin, which are unknown in any other group of animals. Between the extended wing of the Albatross, measuring eleven feet in spread, and the condition in the Kiwi of New Zealand, in which the wing is vanishing, there is every possible variation in size and form. As a rule, the larger the animal the smaller is the wing area. The problem of the origin of the bird's wing is not to be explained by study of existing animals; for the rowing organ of the Penguin, which in itself would never suggest flight, becomes an organ of flight in other birds by the growth upon it of suitable feathers. Anyone who has seen the birds named Divers feeding under water, swimming rapidly with their wings, might never suspect that they were also organs of aerial flight. The Ostrich is even more interesting, for it has not developed flight, and still retains at the extremities of two of the digits the slender claws of a limb which was originally no wing at all, but the support of a four-footed animal (Fig. 46, p. 130).

FLYING MAMMALS

Flight is also developed among mammals. The Insectivora include several interesting examples of animals which are capable of a certain motion through the air. In the tropical forests of the Malay Archipelago are animals known as Flying Squirrels, Flying Opossums, Flying Lemurs, Flying Foxes, in which the skin extends outward laterally from the sides of the body so as to connect the fore limbs with the hind limbs, and is also prolonged backward from the hind limbs to the tail. The four digits are never elongated; the bones of the fore limb are neither longer nor larger than those of the hind limb, and the foot terminates in five little claws as in other four-footed animals. This condition is adapted for the arboreal life which those animals live, leaping from branch to branch, feeding on fruits and leaves, and in some cases upon insects. These mammals may be compared with the Flying Geckos among reptiles in their parachute-like support by extension of the skin, which gives them one of the conditions of support which contribute to constitute flight.

Bats.--One entire order of mammals--the Bats--not only possess true wings, but are capable of flight which is sustained, and in some cases powerful. The wings are clothed with short hair like the rest of the body, and thus the instrument of flight is unlike that of a bird. The flight of a Bat differs from that of all other animals in being dependent upon a modification of the bones of the fore limb, which, without interfering with the animal's movements as a quadruped, secures an extension of the wing which is not inferior in area to that which the bird obtains by elongation of the bones of the arm and fore-arm and its feathers. The distinctive peculiarity of the Bat's wing is in the circumstance that four of the digits of the hand have their bones prolonged to a length which is often equal to the combined length of the arm and fore-arm. The bones of the digits diverge like the ribs of an umbrella, and between them is the wing membrane, which extends from the sides of the body outward, unites the fore limb with the hind limb, and is prolonged down the tail as in the Flying Foxes. Bats have a small membrane in front of the bones of the arm and fore-arm stretching between the shoulder and the wrist, which corresponds with the wing membrane of a bird; but the remainder of the membranes in Bats' wings are absent in birds, because their function is performed by feathers which give the wing its area. The elongated digits of the Bat's wing are folded together and carried at the sides of the body as though they were a few quill pens attached to its wrist, where the one digit, which is applied to the ground in walking, terminates in a claw.

The organs which support animals in the air are thus seen to be more or less dissimilar in each of the great groups of animals. They fall into three chief types: first, the parachute; secondly, the wing due to the feathers appended to the skin; and thirdly, the wing formed of membrane, supported by enormous elongation of the small bones of the back of the hand and fingers. The two types of true wings are limited to birds and bats; and no living reptile approximates to developing such an organ of flight as a wing. Judged, therefore, by the method of comparing the anatomical structures of one animal with another, which is termed "comparative anatomy," the existence of flying reptiles might be pronounced impossible. But in the light which the revelations of geology afford, our convictions become tempered with modesty; and we learn that with Nature nothing is impossible in development of animal structure.

CHAPTER V

DISCOVERY OF THE PTERODACTYLE

Late in the eighteenth century, in 1784, a small fossil animal with wings began to be known through the writings of Collini, as found in the white lithographic limestone of Solenhofen in Bavaria, and was regarded by him as a former inhabitant of the sea. The foremost naturalist of the time, the citizen Cuvier--for it was in the days of the French Republic--in 1801, in lucid language, interpreted the animal as a genus of Saurians. That word, so familiar at the present day, was used in the first half of the century to include Lizards and Crocodiles; and described animals akin to reptiles which were manifestly related neither to Serpents nor Turtles. But the term saurian is no longer in favour, and has faded from science, and is interesting only in ancient history of progress. The lizards soon became classed in close alliance with snakes. And the crocodiles, with the Hatteria, were united with chelonians. Most modern naturalists who use the term saurian still make it an equivalent of lizard, or an animal of the lizard kind.

CUVIER

Cuvier defined this fossil from Solenhofen as distinguished by the extreme elongation of the fourth digit of the hand, and from that character invented for the animal the name Pterodactyle. He tells us that its flight was not due to prolongation of the ribs, as among the living lizards named Dragons; or to a wing formed without the digits being distinguishable from each other, as among Birds; nor with only one digit free from the wing, as among Bats; but by having the wing supported mainly by a single greatly elongated digit, while all the others are short and terminate in claws. Cuvier described the amazing animal in detail, part by part; and such has been the influence of his clear words and fame as a great anatomist that nearly every writer in after-years, in French and in English, repeated Cuvier's conclusion, maintained to the end, that the animal is a saurian.

Long before fashion determined, as an article of educated belief, that fossil animals exist chiefly to bridge over the gaps between those which still survive, the scientific men of Germany were inclined to see in the Pterodactyle such an intermediate type of life. At first Soemmerring and Wagler would have placed the Pterodactyle between mammals and birds.

GOLDFUSS

But the accomplished naturalist Goldfuss, who described another fine skeleton of a Pterodactyle in 1831, saw in this flying animal an indication of the course taken by Nature in changing the reptilian organisation to that of birds and mammals. It is the first flash of light on a dark problem, and its brilliance of inference has never been equalled. Its effects were seen when Prince Charles Bonaparte, the eminent ornithologist, in Italy, suggested for the group the name Ornithosauria; when the profound anatomist de Blainville, in France, placed the short-tailed animal in a class between Reptiles and Birds named Pterodactylia; and Andreas Wagner, of Munich, who had more Pterodactyles to judge from than his predecessors, saw in the fossil animal a saurian in transition to a bird.

VON MEYER

But the German interpretation is not uniform, and Hermann von Meyer, the banker-naturalist of Frankfurt a./M., who made himself conversant with all that his predecessors knew, and enlarged knowledge of the Pterodactyles on the most critical facts of structure, continued to regard them as true reptiles, but flying reptiles. Such is the influence of von Meyer that all parts of the world have shown a disposition to reflect his opinions, especially as they practically coincide with the earlier teaching of Cuvier. Owen and Huxley in England, Cope and Marsh in America, Gaudry in France, and Zittel in Germany have all placed the Pterodactyles as flying reptiles. Their judgment is emphatic. But there is weight of competent opinion to endorse the evolutionary teaching of Goldfuss that they rise above reptiles. To form an independent opinion the modern student must examine the animals, weigh their characters bone by bone, familiarise himself, if possible, with some of the rocks in which they are found; to comprehend the conditions under which the fossils are preserved, which have added not a little to the interest in Pterodactyles, and to the difficulty of interpretation.

GEOLOGICAL HISTORY OF PTERODACTYLES IN GERMANY

We may briefly recapitulate the geological history. Those remains of Ornithosaurs which have been mentioned, with a multitude of others which are the glory of the museums of Munich, Stuttgart, Tuebingen, Heidelberg, Bonn, Haarlem, and London, have all been found in working the lithographic stone of Bavaria. The whitish yellow limestone forms low, flat-topped hills, now isolated from each other by natural denudation, which has removed the intervening rock. The stone is found at some distance north of the Danube, in a line due north of Augsburg, in the country about Pappenheim, and especially at the villages of Solenhofen, Eichstaedt, Kelheim, and Nusplingen. These beds belong to the rocks which are named White Jura limestone in Germany, which is of about the same geological age as the Kimeridge clay in England. Much of it divides into very thin layers, and in these planes of separation the fossils are found. They include the Ammonites lithographicus and a multitude of marine shells, king crabs and other Crustacea, sea-urchins, and other fossils, showing that the deposit was formed in the sea. The preservation of jelly-fish, which so soon disappear when left dry on the beach, shows that the ancient calcareous mud had unusual power of preserving fossils. Into this sea, with its fishes great and small, came land plants from off the land, dragonflies and other insects, tortoises and lizards, Pterodactyles with their flying organs, and birds still clothed with feathers. Sometimes the wing membranes of the flying reptiles are found fully stretched by the wing finger, as in examples to be seen at Munich and in the Yale Museum in Newhaven, in America. At Haarlem there is an example in which the wing membrane appears to be folded much as in the wing of a Bat, when the animal hangs suspended, with the flying membrane bent into a few wide undulations.

The Solenhofen Slate belongs to about the middle period of the history of flying reptiles, for they range through the Secondary epochs of geological time. Remains are recorded in Germany from the Keuper beds at the top of the Trias, which is the bottom division of the Secondary strata; and I believe I have seen fragments of their bones from the somewhat older Muschelkalk of Germany.

THEIR HISTORY IN ENGLAND

In England the remains are found for the first time in the Lower Lias of Lyme Regis, in Dorset, and the Upper Lias of Whitby, in Yorkshire. In Wuertemberg they occur on the same horizons. They reappear in England, in every subsequent age, when the conditions of the strata and their fossils give evidence of near proximity to land. In the Stonesfield Slate of Stonesfield, in Oxfordshire, the bones are found isolated, but indicate animals of some size, though not so large as the rare bones of reputed true birds which appear to have left their remains in the same deposit.

At least two Pterodactyles are found in the Oxford clay, known from more or less fragmentary remains or isolated bones; just as they occur in the Kimeridge Clay, Purbeck Limestone, Wealden sandstones, and especially in newer Secondary rocks, named Gault, Upper Greensand, and Chalk, in the south-east of England.

Owing to exceptional facilities for collecting, in consequence of the Cambridge Greensand being excavated for the valuable mineral phosphate of lime it contains, more than a thousand bones are preserved, more or less broken and battered, in the Woodwardian Museum of the University of Cambridge alone. To give some idea of their abundance, it may be stated that they were mostly gathered during two or three years, as a matter of business, by an intelligent foreman of washers of the nodules of phosphate of lime, which, in commerce, are named coprolites. He soon learned to distinguish Pterodactyle bones from other fossils by their texture, and learned the anatomical names of bones from specimens in the University Museum. This workman, Mr. Pond, employed by Mr. William Farren, brought together not only the best of the remains at Cambridge, but most of those in the museums at York and in London, and the thousands of less perfect specimens in public and private collections which passed through the present writer's hands in endeavours to secure for the University useful illustrations of the animal's structure. These fragments, among which there are few entire bones, are valuable, for they have afforded opportunities of examining the articular ends of bones in every aspect, which is not possible when similar organic remains are embedded in rock in their natural connexions.

In England Flying Reptiles disappear with the Chalk. In that period they were widely distributed, being found in Bohemia, in Brazil, and Kansas in the United States, as well as in Kent and other parts of England. They attained their largest dimensions in this period of geological time. One imperfect fragment of a bone from the Laramie rocks of Canada was described, I believe, by Cope, though not identified by him as Ornithosaurian, and is probably newer than other remains.

ASPECT OF PTERODACTYLES

If this series of animals could all be brought together they would vary greatly in aspect and stature, as well as in structure. Some have the head enormously long, in others it is large and deep, characters which are shared by extinct reptiles which do not fly, and to which some birds may approximate; while in a few the head is small and compact, no more conspicuous, relatively, than the head of a Sparrow. The neck may be slender like that of a Heron, or strong like that of an Eagle; the back is always short, and the tail may be inconspicuous, or as long as the back and neck together. These flying reptiles frequently have the proportions of the limbs similar to those of a Bat, with fore legs strong and hind legs relatively small; while in some the limbs are as long, proportionately, and graceful as those of a Deer. With these differences in proportions of the body are associated great differences in the relative length of the wing and spread of the wing membranes.

DIMENSIONS OF THE ANIMALS

The dimensions of the animals have probably varied in all periods of geological time. The smallest, in the Lithographic Slate, are smaller than Sparrows, while associated with them are others in which the drumstick bone of the leg is eight inches long. In the Cambridge Greensand and Chalk imperfect specimens occur, showing that the upper arm bones are larger than those of an Ox. The shaft is one and a half inches in diameter and the ends three inches wide. Such remains may indicate Pterodactyles not inferior in size to the extinct Moas of New Zealand, but with immensely larger heads, animals far larger than birds of flight.

The late Sir Richard Owen, on first seeing these fragmentary remains, said "the flying reptile with outstretched pinions must have appeared like the soaring Roc of Arabian romance, but with the features of leathern wings with crooked claws superinduced, and gaping mouth with threatening teeth." Eventually we shall obtain more exact ideas of their aspect, when the structures of the several regions of the body have been examined. The great dimensions of the stretch of wing, often computed at twenty feet in the larger examples, might lead to expectations of great weight of body, if it were not known that an albatross, with wings spreading eleven feet, only weighs about seventeen pounds.

CHAPTER VI

HOW ANIMALS ARE INTERPRETED BY THEIR BONES

There is only one safe path which the naturalist may follow who would tell the story of the meaning and nature of an extinct type of animal life, and that is to compare it as fully as possible in its several bones, and as a whole, with other animals, especially with those which survive. It is easy to fix the place in nature of living animals and determine their mutual relations to each other, because all the organs--vital as well as locomotive--are available for comparison. On such evidence they are grouped together into the large divisions of Beasts, Birds, and Reptiles; as well as placed in smaller divisions termed Orders, which are based upon less important modifications of fundamental structures. All these characteristic organs have usually disappeared in the fossil. Hence a new method of study of the hard parts of the skeleton, which alone are preserved, is used in the endeavour to discover how the Flying Reptile or other extinct animal is to be classified, and how it acquired its characters or came into existence.

VARIATIONS OF BONES AMONG MAMMALIA

Resemblances and differences in the bones are easily over-estimated in importance as evidence of pedigree relationship. The Mammalia show, by means of such skeletons as are exhibited in any Natural History Museum, how small is the importance to be attached to even the existence of any group of bones in determining its grade of organisation. The whole Whale tribe suckle their young and conform to the distinctive characters in brain and lungs which mark them as being mammals. But if there is one part of the skeleton more than another which distinguishes the Mammalia, it is the girdle of bones at the hips which supports the hind limbs. It is characterised by the bone named the ilium being uniformly directed forward. Yet in the Whale tribe the hip-girdle and the hind limb which it usually supports are so faintly indicated as to be practically lost; while the fore limb becomes a paddle without distinction of digits, and is therefore devoid of hoofs or claws, which are usual terminations of the extremities in mammals. Yet this swimming paddle, with its ill-defined bones--sometimes astonishing in number, as well as in fewness of the finger bones--is represented by the burrowing fore limb of the Mole, which lives underground; by the elongated hoofed legs of the Giraffe, which lives on plains; and the extended arm and finger bones of the Bat, which are equally mammals with the Whale. From such comparison it is seen that no proportion, or form, or length, or use of the bones of the limbs, or even the presence of limbs, is necessarily characteristic of a mammal. No limitation can be placed upon the possible diversity of form or development of bones in unknown animals, when they are considered in the light of such experience of varied structural conditions in living members of a single class.

What is true for the limbs and the bony arches which support them is true for the backbone also, for the ribs, and to some extent for the skull. The neck in the Whale is shortened almost beyond recognition. In the Giraffe the same seven vertebrae are elongated into a marvellous neck; so that in the technical definition of a mammal both are said to have seven neck vertebrae. Yet exceptions show a capacity for variation. One of the Sloths reduces the number to six, while another has nine vertebrae in the neck; proving that there is no necessary difference between a mammal and a reptile when judged by a character which is typically so distinctive of mammals as the number of the neck bones.

The skull varies too, though to a less extent. The Great Ant-eater of South America is a mammal absolutely without teeth. The Porpoises have a simple unvarying row of conical teeth with single roots extending along the jaw. And the dental armature of the jaws, and relative dimensions of the skull bones, exhibit such diversity, in evidence of what may be parted with or acquired, that recognition of the many reptilian structures and bones in the skull of Ornithorhynchus, the Australian Duckbill, demonstrates that the difficulties in recognising an animal by its bones are real, unless we can discover the Animal Type to which the bones belong; and that there is very little in osteology which may not be lost without affecting an animal's grade of organisation.

VARIATION IN SKIN COVERING OF MAMMALS

Even the covering of the body varies in the same class, or even order of animals, so that the familiar growth on the skin is never its only possible covering. The Indian ant-eater, named Manis, which looks like a gigantic fir-cone, the Armadillo, which sheathes the body in rings of bone, bearing only a scanty development of hair, are examples of mammalian hair, as singular as the quills of a Porcupine, the horn of a Rhinoceros, or the growth of hair of varying length and stoutness on different parts of the body in various animals, or the imperfect development of hair in the marine Cetacea. Among living animals it is enough for practical purposes to say that a mammal is clothed with hair, but in a fossil state the hair must usually be lost beyond recognition from its fineness and shortness of growth.

VARIATION IN SKIN COVERING OF BIRDS

No Class of living animals is more homogeneous than Birds; and well-preserved remains prove that, at least as far back in time as the Upper Oolites, birds were clothed with feathers of essentially the same mode of growth and appearance as the feathers of living birds. There may, therefore, be no ground for assuming that the covering was ever different, though some regions of the skin are free from feathers. Yet the variations from fine under-down to the scale-like feathers on the wings of a Penguin, or the great feathers in the wings of birds of flight, or the double quill of the Ostrich group, are calculated to yield dissimilar impressions in a fossil state, even if the fine down would be preserved in any stratum.

VARIATION IN THE BONES OF BIRDS

Osteologically there is less variety in the skeleton of birds than in other great groups of animals. The existing representatives do not exhaust its capability for modification. The few specimens of birds hitherto found in the Secondary strata have rudely removed many differences in the bones which separated living birds from reptiles; so that if only the older fossil birds were known, and the Tertiary and living birds had not existed, a bird might have been defined as an animal having its jaw armed with teeth, instead of devoid of teeth; with vertebrae cupped at both ends, instead of with a saddle-shaped articulation which in front is concave from side from side, and convex from above downwards; in which the bones of the hand are separate, so that three digits terminating in claws can be applied to the ground, instead of the metacarpal bones being united in a solid mass with clawless digits; and in which the tail is elongated like the tail of a lizard. Yet the limits to variation are not to be formulated till Nature has exhausted all her resources in efforts to preserve organic types by adapting them to changed circumstances. Birds may be regarded theoretically as equally capable with mammals of parting with almost every distinctive structure in the skeleton by which it is best known. Even the living frigate bird blends the early joints of the backbone into a compact mass like a sacrum. The Penguin has a cup-and-ball articulation in the early dorsal vertebrae, with the ball in front. And the genus Cypselus has the upper arm bone almost as broad as long, unlike the bird type. Such examples prove that we are apt to accept the predominant structures in an animal type as though they were universal, and forget that inferences based, like those of early investigators, on limited materials may be re-examined with advantage.

VARIATION IN THE BONES OF REPTILES

The true Reptilia, notwithstanding some strong resemblances to Birds in technical characters of the skeleton, display among their surviving representatives an astonishing diversity in the bony framework of the body, exceeding that of the mammalia. This unlooked-for capacity for varying the plan of construction of the skeleton is in harmony with the diversity of structure in groups of extinct animals to which the name reptiles has also been given. The interval in form is so vast between Serpent and Tortoise, and so considerable in structure of the skeleton between these and the several groups of Lizards, Crocodiles, and Hatteria, that any other diversity could not be more surprising. And the inference is reasonable that just as mammals live in the air, in the sea, on the earth, and burrow under the earth, similar modes of existence might be expected for birds and reptiles, though no bird is yet known to have put on the aspect of a fish, and no reptiles have been discovered which roamed in herds like antelopes, or lived in the air like birds or bats, unless these fossil flying animals prove on examination to justify the name by which they are known.

Comparative study of structure in this way demolishes the prejudice, born of experience of the life which now remains on earth, that the ideas of Reptile and of Flight are incongruous, and not to be combined in one animal. The comparative study of the parts of animals does not leave the student in a chaos of possibilities, but teaches us that organic structures, which mark the grades of life, have only a limited scope of change; while Nature flings away every part of the skeleton which is not vital, or changes its form with altering circumstances of existence, enforced by revolutions of the Earth's surface in geological time, in her efforts to save organisms from extinction and pass the grade of life onward to a later age.

The bones are only of value to the naturalist as symbols, inherited or acquired, and vary in value as evidence of the nature and association of those vital organs which differentiate the great groups of the vertebrata.

These distinctive structures, which separate Mammals, Birds, and Reptiles, are sometimes demonstrated by the impress of their existence left on the bones; or sometimes they may be inferred from the characters of the skeleton as a whole.

CHAPTER VII

INTERPRETATION OF PTERODACTYLES BY THEIR SOFT PARTS

THE ORGANS WHICH FIX AN ANIMAL'S PLACE IN NATURE

We shall endeavour to ascertain what marks of its grade of organisation the Pterodactyle has to show. The organs which are capable of modifying the bones are probably limited to the kidneys, the brain, and the organs of respiration. It may be sufficient to examine the latter two.

PNEUMATIC FORAMINA IN PTERODACTYLES

Hermann von Meyer, the historian of the Ornithosaurs of the Lithographic Slate, as early as 1837 described some Pterodactyle bones from the Lias of Franconia, which showed that air was admitted into the interior of the bones by apertures near their extremities, which, from this circumstance, are known as pneumatic foramina. He drew the inference, naturally enough, that such a structure is absolute proof that the Pterodactyle was a flying animal. It was not quite the right form in which the conclusion should have been stated, because the Ostrich and other birds which do not fly have the principal bones pneumatic. Afterwards, in 1859, the larger bones which Professor Sedgwick, of Cambridge, transmitted to Sir Richard Owen established this condition as characteristic of the Flying Reptiles of the Cambridge Greensand. It was thus found as a distinctive structure of the bones both at the beginning and the close of the geological history of these animals. Von Meyer remarks that the supposition readily follows that in the respiratory process there was some similarity between Pterodactyles and Birds. This cautious statement may perhaps be due to the circumstance that in many animals air cavities are developed in the skull without being connected with organs of respiration. It is well known that the bulk of the Elephant's head is due to the brain cavity being protected with an envelope formed of large air cells. Small air cells are seen in the skulls of oxen, pigs, and many other mammals, as well as in the human forehead. The head of a bird like the Owl owes something of its imposing appearance to the way in which its mass is enlarged by the dense covering of air cells in the bones above the brain, like that seen in some Cretaceous Pterodactyles. Nor are the skulls of Crocodiles or Tortoises exceptions to the general rule that an animal's head bones may be pneumatic without implying a pneumatic prolongation of air from the lungs. The mere presence of air cells without specification of the region of the skeleton in which they occur is not remarkable. The holes by which air enters the bones are usually much larger in Pterodactyles than in Birds, but the entrance to the air cell prolonged into the bones is the same in form and position in both groups. So far as can be judged by this character, there is no difference between them. The importance of the comparison can only be appreciated by examining the bones side by side. In the upper arm bone of a bird, on what is known as the ulnar border, near to the shoulder joint, and on the side nearest to it, is the entrance to the air cell in the humerus. In the Pterodactyle the corresponding foramen has the same position, form, and size, and is not one large hole, but a reticulation of small perforations, one beyond another, exactly such as are seen in the entrance to the air cell in the bone of a bird, in which the pneumatic character is found. For it is not every bird of flight which has this pneumatic condition of the bones; and Dr. Crisp stated that quite a number of birds--the Swallow, Martin, Snipe, Canary, Wood-wren and Willow-wren, Whinchat, Glossy-starling, Spotted-fly-catcher, and Black-headed Bunting--have no air in their bones. And it is well known that in many birds, especially water birds, it is only the upper bones of the limbs which are pneumatic, while the smaller bones retain the marrow.

LUNGS AND AIR CELLS

It may be well to remember that the lungs of a bird are differently conditioned from those of any other animal. Instead of hanging freely suspended in the cone-shaped chamber of the thorax formed by the ribs and sternum, they are firmly fixed on each side, so that the ribs deeply indent them and hold them in place. The lungs have the usual internal structure, being made up of branching cells. The chief peculiarity consists in the way in which the air passes not only into them, but through them. The air tube of the throat of a bird, unlike that of a man, has the organ of voice, not at the upper end in the form of a larynx, but at the lower end, forming what is termed a syrinx. There is no evidence of this in a fossil state, although in a few birds the rings of the trachaea become ossified, and are preserved. But below the syrinx the trachaea divides into two bronchi, tubes which carry the ringed character into the lungs for some distance, and these give off branches termed bronchial tubes, the finer subdivisions from which, in their clustered minute branching sacs, make up the substance of the lung. There is nothing exceptional in that. But towards the outer or middle part of the ventral or under surface of the lungs, four or five rounded openings are seen on each side. Each of these openings resembles the entrance of the air cell into a bone, since it displays several smaller openings which lead to it. Each opening from the lung leads to an air cell. Those cells may be regarded as the blowing out of the membrane which covers the lungs into a film which holds air like a mass of soap bubbles, until the whole cavity of the body of a bird from neck to tail is occupied by sacculated air cells, commonly ten in number, five on each side, though two frequently blend at the base of the neck in the region of the #V#-shaped bone named the clavicle or furculum, popularly known as the merry-thought. Most people have seen some at least of these semi-transparent bladder-like air cells beneath the skin in the abdominal region of a fowl. The cells have names from their positions, and on each side one is abdominal, two are thoracic, one clavicular, and one cervical, which last is at the base of the neck. The clavicular and abdominal air cells are perhaps the most interesting. The air cell termed clavicular sends a process outward towards the arm, along with the blood vessels which supply the arm. Thus this air cell, entering the region of the axilla or arm-pit, enters the upper arm bone usually on its under side, close to the articular head of the humerus, and in the same way the air may pass from bone to bone through every bone in the fore limb. The hind limbs similarly receive air from the abdominal air cell, which supplies the femur and other bones of the leg, the sacrum, and the tail. But the joints of the backbone in front of the sacrum receive their air from the cervical air sac. The air cells are not limited to the bones, but ramify through the body, and in some cases extend among the muscles. A bird may be said to breathe not only with its lungs, but with its whole body. And it is even affirmed that respiration has been carried on through a broken arm bone when the throat was closed, and the bird under water.

Birds differ greatly in the extent to which the aircell system prolonged from the lungs is developed, some having the air absent from every bone, while others, like the Swift, are reputed to have air in every bone of the body.

Comparison shows that in so far as the bones are the same in Bird and Ornithosaur, the evidence of the air cells entering them extends to resemblance, if not coincidence, in every detail. No living group of animals except birds has pneumatic limb bones, in relation to the lungs; so that it is reasonable to conclude that the identical structures in the bones were due to the same cause in both the living and extinct groups of animals. It is impossible to say that the lungs were identical in Birds and Pterodactyles, but so far as evidence goes, there is no ground for supposing them to have been different.

THE LUNGS OF REPTILES

There is nothing comparable to birds, either in the lungs of living reptiles or in their relation to the bones. The Chameleon is remarkable in that the lung is not a simple bladder prolonged through the whole length of the body cavity, as in a serpent, but it develops a number of large lateral branches visible when the body is laid open. Except near the trachaea, where the tissue has the usual density of a lizard lung, the air cell is scarcely more complicated than the air bladder of a fish, and does not enter into any bone of the skeleton. And although many fishes like the Loach have the swim bladder surrounded by bone connected with the head, it offers no analogy to the pneumatic condition of the bones in the Pterodactyle.

THE FORM OF THE BRAIN CAVITY

But the identity of the pneumatic foramina in Birds and Flying Reptiles is not a character which stands by itself as evidence of organisation, for a mould of the form of the brain case contributes evidence of another structural condition which throws some light on the nature of Ornithosaurs. Among many of the lower animals, such as turtles, the brain does not fill the chamber in the dry skull, in which the same bones are found as are moulded upon the brain in higher animals. For the brain case in such reptiles is commonly an envelope of cartilage, as among certain fishes; and except among serpents, the Ophidia, the bones do not completely close the reptilian brain case in front. The brain fills the brain case completely among birds. A mould from its interior is almost as definite in displaying the several parts of which it is formed as the actual brain would be. And the chief regions of the brain in a bird--cerebrum, optic lobes, cerebellum--show singularly little variation in proportion or position. The essential fact in a bird's brain, which separates it absolutely from all other animals, is that the pair of nerve masses known as the optic lobes are thrust out at the sides, so that the large cerebral hemispheres extend partly over them as they extend between them to abut against the cerebellum. This remarkable condition has no parallel among other vertebrate animals. In Fishes, Amphibians, Reptiles, and Mammals the linear succession of the several parts of the brain is never departed from; and any appearance of variation from it among mammals is more apparent than real, for the linear succession may be seen in the young calf till the cerebral hemispheres grow upward and lop backward, so as to hide the relatively small brain masses which correspond to the optic lobes of reptiles, extending over these corpora-quadrigemina, as they are named, so as to cover more or less of the mass of the cerebellum. From these conditions of the brain and skull, it would not be possible to mistake a mould from the brain case of a bird for that of a reptile, though in some conditions of preservation it is conceivable that the mould of the brain of a bird might be distinguished with difficulty from that of the brain in the lowest mammals. Taken by itself, the avian form of brain in an animal would be as good evidence that its grade of organisation was that of a bird as could be offered.

THE BRAIN IN SOLENHOFEN PTERODACTYLES

It happens that moulds of the brain of Pterodactyles, more or less complete, are met with of all geological ages--Liassic, Oolitic, and Cretaceous. The Solenhofen Slate is the only deposit in Europe in which Pterodactyle skulls can be said to be fairly numerous. They commonly have the bones so thin as to show the form of the upper surface of the mould of the brain, or the bones have scaled off the mould, or remain in the counterpart slab of stone, so as to lay bare the shape of the brain mass.

In the Museum at Heidelberg a skull of this kind is seen in the long-tailed genus of Pterodactyles named Rhamphorhynchus. It shows the large rounded cerebral hemispheres, which extend in front of cerebral masses of smaller size a little below them in position, which perhaps are as like the brain of a monotreme mammal as a bird.

The short-tailed Pterodactylus described by Cuvier has the cerebral hemispheres very similar to those of a bird, but the relations of the hinder parts of the brain to each other are less clear.

The first specimen to show the back of the brain was found by Mr. John Francis Walker, M.A., in the Cambridge Greensand. I was able to remove the thick covering of cellular bone which originally extended above it, and thus expose evidence that in the mutual relations of the fore and hind parts of the brain bird and ornithosaur were practically identical. Another Cambridge Greensand skull showed that in the genus Ornithocheirus the optic lobes of the brain are developed laterally, as in birds. That skull was isolated and imperfect. But about the same time the late Rev. W. Fox, of Brixton, in the Isle of Wight, obtained from Wealden beds another skull, with jaws, teeth, and the principal bones of the skeleton, which showed that the Wealden Pterodactyle Ornithodesmus had a similar and bird-like brain. In 1888 Mr. E. T. Newton, F.R.S., obtained a skull from the Upper Lias, uncrushed and free from distortion. This made known the natural mould of the brain, which shows the cerebral hemispheres, optic lobes, and cerebellum more distinctly than in the specimens previously known. In some respects it recalls the Heidelberg brain of Rhamphorhynchus in the apparently transverse subdivision of the optic lobes, but it is unmistakably bird-like, and quite unlike any reptile.

IMPORTANCE OF THE BRAIN AND BREATHING ORGANS

So far as the evidence goes, it appears that these fossil flying animals show no substantial differences from birds, either in the mould of the brain or the impress of the breathing organs upon the bones. These approximations to birds of the nervous and respiratory systems, which are beyond question two of the most important of the vital organs of an animal, and distinctive beyond all others of birds, place the naturalist in a singular dilemma. He must elect whether he will trust his interpretation to the soft organs, which among existing animals never vary their type in the great classes of vertebrate animals, and on which the animal is defined as something distinct from its envelope the skeleton and its appendages the limbs, or whether he will ignore them. The answer must choose substantially between belief that the existing order of Nature gives warrant for believing that these vital characteristics which have been discussed might equally coexist with the skeleton of a mammal or a reptile, as with that of a bird, for which there is no particle of evidence in existing life. Or, as an alternative, the fact must be accepted that birds only have such vital organs as are here found, and therefore the skeleton, that may be associated with them, cannot affect the reference of the type to the same division of the animal kingdom as birds. The decision need not be made without further consideration. But brain and breathing organs of the avian type are structures of a different order of stability in most animals from the bones, which vary to a remarkable extent in almost every ordinal group of animals.

TEMPERATURE OF THE BLOOD

The organs of circulation and digestion are necessarily unknown. There are reasons why the blood may have been hot, such as the evidences from the wings of exceptional activity; though the temperature depends more upon the amount of blood in the body than upon the apparatus by which it is distributed. We speak of a Crocodile as cold-blooded, yet it is an animal with a four-chambered heart not incomparable with that of a bird. On the other hand, the Tunny, a sort of giant Mackerel, is a fish with a three-chambered heart, only breathing the air dissolved in water, which has blood as warm as a mammal, its temperature being compared to that of a pig. Several fishes have blood as warm as that of Manis, the scaly ant-eater; and many birds have hotter blood than mammals. The term "hot-blooded," as distinct from "cold-blooded," applied to animals, is relative to the arbitrary human standard of experience, and expresses no more than the circumstance that mammals and birds are warmer animals than reptiles and fishes.

The exceptional temperature of the Flying Fish has led to a vague impression that physical activity and its effect upon the amount of blood which vigour of movement circulates, are more important in raising an animal's temperature than possession of the circulatory organs commonly associated with hot blood, which drive the blood in distinct courses through the body and breathing organs. Yet the kind of heart which is always associated with vital structures such as Pterodactyles are inferred to have possessed from the brain mould and the pneumatic foramina in the bones, is the four-chambered heart of the bird and the mammal. Considering these organs alone--of which the fossil bones yield evidence--we might anticipate, by the law of known association of structures, that nothing distinctly reptilian existed in the other soft part of the vital organisation, because there is no evidence in favour of or against such a possibility.

CHAPTER VIII

THE PLAN OF THE SKELETON

While these animals are incontestably nearer to birds than to any other animals in their plan of organisation, thus far no proof has been found that they are birds, or can be included in the same division of vertebrate life with feathered animals. It is one of the oldest and soundest teachings of Linnaeus that a bird is known by its feathers; and the record is a blank as to any covering to the skin in Pterodactyles. There is the strongest probability against feathers having existed such as are known in the Archaeopteryx, because every Solenhofen Ornithosaur appears to have the body devoid of visible or preservable covering, while the two birds known from the Solenhofen Slate deposit are well clothed with feathers in perfect preservation. We turn from the skin to the skeleton.

The plan on which the skeleton is constructed remains as evidence of the animal's place in nature, which is capable of affording demonstration on which absolute reliance would have been placed, if the brain and pneumatic foramina had remained undiscovered. With the entire skeleton before us, it is inconceivable that anatomical science should fail to discover the true nature of the animal to which it belonged, by the method of comparing one animal with another. There is no lack of this kind of evidence of Pterodactyles in the three or four scores of skeletons, and thousands of isolated or associated bones, preserved in the public museums of Europe and America.

I may recall the circumstance that the discovery of skeletons of fossil animals has occasionally followed upon the interpretation of a single fragment, from which the animal has been well defined, and sometimes accurately drawn, before it was ever seen. So I propose, before drawing any conclusions from the skeletons in the entirety of their construction, to examine them bone by bone, and region by region, for evidence that will manifest the nature of this brood of Dragons. Their living kindred, and perhaps their extinct allies, assembled as a jury, may be able to determine whether resemblances exist between them, and whether such similarity between the bones as exists is a common inheritance, or is a common acquisition due to similar ways of life, and no evidence of the grade of the organism among vertebrate animals.

The bones of these Ornithosaurs, when found isolated, first have to be separated from the organisms with which they are associated and mixed in the geological strata. This discrimination is accomplished in the first instance by means of the texture of the surface. The density and polish of the bones is even more marked than in the bones of birds, and is usually associated with a peculiar thinness of substance of the bone, which is comparable to the condition in a bird, though usually a little stouter, so that the bones resist crushing better. Pterodactyle bones in many instances are recognised by their straightness and comparatively uniform dimensions, due to the exceptional number of long bones which enter into the structure of the wing as compared with birds. When the bones are unerringly determined as Ornithosaurian, they are placed side by side with all the bones which are most like them, till, judged by the standard of the structures of living animals, the fossil is found to show a composite construction as though it were not one animal but many, while its individual bones often show equally composite characters, as though parts of the corresponding bone in several animals had been cunningly fitted together and moulded into shape.

THE PLAN OF THE HEAD IN ORNITHOSAURS

The head is always the most instructive part of an animal. It is less than an inch long in the small Solenhofen skeleton named Pterodactylus brevirostris, and is said to be three feet nine inches long in the toothless Pterodactyle Ornithostoma from the Chalk of Kansas. Most of these animals have a long, slender, conical form of head, tapering to the point like the beak of a Heron, forming a long triangle when seen from above or from the side. Sometimes the head is depressed in front, with the beak flattened or rounded as in a Duck or Goose, and occasionally in some Wealden and Greensand species the jaws are truncated in front in a massive snout quite unlike any bird. The back of the head is sometimes rounded as among birds, showing a smooth pear-shaped posterior convexity in the region of the brain. Sometimes the back of the head is square and vertical or oblique. Occasionally a great crest of cellular tissue is extended backward from above the brain case over the spines of the neck bones.

There are always from two to four lateral openings in the skull. First, the nostril is nearest to the extremity of the beak. Secondly, the orbits of the eyes are placed far backward. These two openings are always present. The nostril may incline upward. The orbits of the eyes are usually lateral, though their upper borders sometimes closely approximate, as in the woodpecker-like types from the Solenhofen Slate named Pterodactylus Kochi, now separated as another genus. In most genera there is an opening in the side of the head, between the eye hole and the nostril, known as the antorbital vacuity; and another opening, which is variable in size and known as the temporal vacuity, is placed behind the eye. The former is common in the skulls of birds, the latter is absent from all birds and found in many reptiles.

The palate is usually imperfectly seen, but English and American specimens have shown that it has much in common with the palate in birds, though it varies greatly in form of the bones in representatives from the Lias, Oolites, and Cretaceous rocks.

From the scientific aspect the relative size of the head, its form, and the positions and dimensions of its apertures and processes, are of little importance in comparison with its plan of construction, as evidenced by the positions and relations to each other of the bones of which it is formed. There usually is some difficulty in stating the limits of the bones of the skull, because in Pterodactyles, as among birds, they usually blend together, so that in the adult animal the sutures between the bones are commonly obliterated.

Bones have relations to each other and places in the head which can only change as the organs with which they are associated change their positions. No matter what the position of a nostril may be--at the extremity of a long snout, as in an ant-eater, or far back at the top of the head in a porpoise, or at the side of the head in a bird--it is always bordered by substantially the same bones, which vary in length and size with the changing place of the nostril and the form of the head. Every region of the head is defined by this method of construction; so that eye holes and nose holes, brain case and jaw bones, palate and teeth, beak, and back of the skull are all instructive to those who seek out the life-history of these animals. We may briefly examine the head of an Ornithosaurian.

BONES ABOUT THE NOSTRIL

No matter what its form may be, the head of an Ornithosaur always terminates in front in a single bone called the intermaxillary. It sends a bar of bone backward above the visible nostrils, between them; and a bar on each side forms the margin of the jaw in which teeth are implanted. The bone varies in depth, length, sharpness, bluntness, slenderness, and massiveness. As the bone becomes long the jaw is compressed from side to side, and the openings of the nostrils are removed backward to an increasing distance from the extremity of the beak.

The outer and hinder border of the nostril is made by another bone named the maxillary bone, which is usually much shorter than the premaxillary. It contains the hindermost teeth, which rarely differ from those in front, except in sometimes being smaller.

The nasal bones, which always make the upper and hinder border of the nostrils, meet each other above them, in the middle line of the beak.

The nostrils are unusually large in the Lias genus named Dimorphodon, and small in species of the genus Rhamphorhynchus from Solenhofen. Such differences result from the relative dimensions and proportions of these three bones which margin the nasal vacuity, and by varying growth of their front margins or of their hinder margins govern the form of the snout.

The jaws are most massive in the genera known from the Wealden beds to the Chalk. The palatal surface is commonly flat or convex, and often marked by an elevated median ridge which corresponds to a groove in the lower jaw, though the median ridge sometimes divides the palate into two parallel concave channels. The jaw is margined with teeth which are rarely fewer than ten or more than twenty on each side. They are sharp, compressed from side to side, curved inward, and never have a saw-like edge on the back and front margins. No teeth occur upon the bones of the palate.

In most birds there is a large vacuity in the side of the head between the nostril and the orbit of the eye, partly separated from it by the bone which carries the duct for tears named the lachrymal bone. The same preorbital vacuity is present in all long-tailed Pterodactyles, though it is either less completely defined or absent in the group with short tails. It affords excellent distinctive characters for defining the genera. In the long-tailed genus Scaphognathus from Solenhofen this preorbital opening is much larger than the nostril, while in Dimorphodon these vacuities are of about equal size. Rhamphorhynchus is distinguished by the small size of the antorbital vacuity, which is placed lower than the nostril on the side of the face. The aperture is always imperfectly defined in Pterodactylus, and is a relatively small vacuity compared with the long nostril. In Ptenodracon the antorbital vacuity appears to have no existence separate from the nostril which adjoins the eye hole. And so far as is known at present there is no lateral opening in advance of the eye in the skull in any Ornithosaur from Cretaceous rocks, though the toothless Ornithostoma is the only genus with the skull complete. When a separate antorbital vacuity exists, it is bordered by the maxillary bone in front, and by the malar bone behind. The prefrontal bone is at its upper angle. That bone is known in a separate state in reptiles and, I think, in monotreme mammals. Its identity is soon lost in the mammal, and its function in the skull is different from the corresponding bone in Pterodactyles.

BONES ABOUT THE EYES

The third opening in the side of the head, counting from before backward, is the orbit of the eye. In this vacuity is often seen the sclerotic circle of overlapping bones formed in the external membrane of the eye, like those in nocturnal birds and some reptiles. The eye hole varies in form from an inverted pear-shape to an oblique or transverse oval, or a nearly circular outline. It is margined by the frontal bone above; the tear bone or lachrymal, and the malar or cheek bone in front; while the bones behind appear to be the quadrato-jugal and post-frontal bones, though the bones about the eye are somewhat differently arranged in different genera.

The eyes were frequently, if not always, in contact with the anterior walls of the brain case, as in many birds, and are always far back in the side of the head. In Dimorphodon they are in front of the articulation of the lower jaw; in Rhamphorhynchus, above that articulation; while in Ornithostoma they are behind the articulation for the jaw. This change is governed by the position of the quadrate bone, which is vertical in the Lias genus, inclined obliquely forward in the fossils from the Oolites, and so much inclined in the Chalk fossil that the small orbit is thrown relatively further back.

Thus far the chief difference in the Pterodactyle skull from that of a bird is in the way in which the malar arch is prolonged backward on each side. It is a slender bar of bone in birds, without contributing ascending processes to border vacuities in the side of the face, while in these fossil animals the lateral openings are partly separated by the ascending processes of these bones. This divergence from birds, in the malar bone entering the orbit of the eye is approximated to among reptiles and mammals, though the conditions, and perhaps the presence of a bone like the post-orbital bone, are paralleled only among Reptiles. The Pterodactyles differ among themselves enough for the head to make a near approach to Reptiles in Dimorphodon, and to Birds in Pterodactylus. In the Ground Hornbill and the Shoebill the lachrymal bones in front of the orbits of the eyes grow down to meet the malar bars without uniting with them. The post-frontal region also is prolonged downward almost as far as the malar bar, as though to show that a bird might have its orbital circle formed in the same way and by the same bones as in Pterodactylus. Cretaceous Ornithosaurs sometimes differ from birds apparently in admitting the quadrato-jugal bone into the orbit. It then becomes an expanded plate, instead of a slender bar as in all birds.

THE TEMPORAL FOSSA

A fourth vacuity is known as the temporal fossa. When the skull of such a mammal as a Rabbit, or Sheep, is seen from above, there is a vacuity behind the orbits for the eyes, which in life is occupied by the muscles which work the lower jaw. It is made by the malar bone extending from the back of the orbit and the process of bone, called the zygomatic process, extending forward from the articulation of the jaw, which arches out to meet the malar bone.

In birds there is no conspicuous temporal fossa, because the malar bar is a slender rod of bone in a line with the lower end of the quadrate bone.

Reptile skulls have sometimes one temporal vacuity on each side, as among tortoises, formed by a single lateral bar. These vacuities, which correspond to those of mammals in position, are seen from the top of the head, as lateral vacuities behind the orbits of the eyes, and are termed superior temporal vacuities. In addition to these there is often in other reptiles a lateral opening behind the eye, termed the inferior temporal vacuity, seen in Crocodiles, in Hatteria, and in Lizards; and in such skulls there are two temporal bars seen in side view, distinguished as superior and inferior. The superior arch always includes the squamosal bone, which is at the back of the single bar in mammals. The lower arch includes the malar bone, which is in front in the single arch of mammals. The circumstance that both these arches are connected with the quadrate bone makes the double temporal arch eminently reptilian.

In Ornithosaurs the lateral temporal vacuity varies from a typically reptilian condition to one which, without becoming avian, approaches the bird type. In skulls from the Lias, Dimorphodon and Campylognathus, there is a close parallel to the living New Zealand reptile Hatteria, in the vertical position of the quadrate bone and in the large size of the vacuity behind and below the eye, which extends nearly the height of the skull. In the species of the genus Pterodactylus, the forward inclination of the quadrate bone recalls the Curlew, Snipe, and other birds. The back of the head is rounded, and the squamosal bone, which appears to enter into the wall of the brain case as in birds and mammals, is produced more outward than in birds, but less than in mammals, so as to contribute a little to the arch which is in the position of the post-frontal bone of reptiles. It is triangular, and stretches from the outer angle of the frontal bone at the back of the orbit to the squamosal behind, where it also meets the quadrate bone. Its third lower branch meets the quadratojugal, which rests upon the front of the quadrate bone, as in Iguanodon, and is unlike Dimorphodon in its connexions. In that genus the supra-temporal bone, or post-orbital bone, appears to rest upon the post-frontal and connect it with the quadrato-jugal. In Dimorphodon the malar bone is entirely removed from the quadrate, but in Pterodactylus it meets its articular end. Between the post-frontal bone above and the quadrato-jugal bone below is a small lunate opening, which represents the lateral temporal vacuity; and so far, this is a reptilian character. But if the thin post-frontal bone were absorbed, Pterodactylus would resemble birds. There is no evidence that the quadrate bone is free in any Ornithosaurs, as it is in all birds, while in Dimorphodon it unites by suture with the squamosal bone. In Ornithostoma the lateral temporal vacuity is little more than a slit between the quadrate bone below, the quadrato-jugal in front, and what may be the post-frontal bone behind (see Fig. 2, p. 12).

BONES ABOUT THE BRAIN

The bones containing the brain appear to be the same as form the brain case in birds. The form of the back of the skull varies in two ways. First it may be flat above and flat at the back, when the back of the head appears to be square. This condition is seen in all the long-tailed genera, such as Campylognathus from the Lias and Rhamphorhynchus, and is associated with a high position for the upper temporal bar. Secondly, the back of the head may be rounded convexly, both above and behind. That condition is seen in the short-tailed genera, such as Pterodactylus. But in the large Cretaceous types, such as Ornithocheirus and Ornithostoma, the superior longitudinal ridge which runs back in the middle line of the face becomes elevated and compressed from side to side at the back of the head as a narrow deep crest, prolonged backward over the neck vertebrae for some inches of length. All these three types are paralleled more or less in birds which have the back of the head square like the Heron, or rounded like the Woodpecker; or crested, though the crest of the Cormorant is not quite identical with Ornithocheirus, being a distinct bone at the back of the head in the bird which never blends with the skull. In so far as the crest is reptilian it suggests the remarkable crest of the Chameleon. In the structure of the back of the skull the bones are a modification of the reptilian type of Hatteria in the Lias genus Campylognathus, but the reptilian characters appear to be lost in the less perfectly preserved skulls of Cretaceous genera.

The palate is well known in the chief groups of Ornithosaurs, such as Campylognathus, Scaphognathus, and Cycnorhamphus.

Mr. E. T. Newton, F.R.S., has shown that in the English skull from the Lias of Whitby, the forms of the bones are similar to the palate in birds and unlike the conditions in reptiles. There is one feature, however, which may indicate a resemblance to Dicynodon and other fossil reptiles from South Africa. A slender bone extends from the base of the brain case, named the basi-sphenoid bone, outward and forward to the inner margin of the quadrate bone (Fig. 22). A bone is found thus placed in those South African Reptiles, which show many resemblances to the Monotreme and Marsupial Mammals. It is not an ordinary element of the skeleton and is unknown in living animals of any kind in that position. It has been thought possible that it may represent one of the bones which among mammals are diminutive and are included in the internal ear. The resemblance may have some interest hereafter, as helping to show that certain affinities of the Ornithosaurs may lie outside the groups of existing reptiles. Instead of being directed transversely outward, as in the palatal region of Dicynodon lacerticeps, they diverge outward and forward to the inner border of the articulation for the lower jaw which is upon the quadrate bone.

BONES OF THE PALATE

There is a pair of bones which extend forward from these inner articular borders of the quadrate bones, and converge in a long #V#-shape till they merge in the hard palate formed by the bones of the front of the beak, named intermaxillary and maxillary bones. The limits of the bones of the palate are not distinct, but there can be no doubt that the front of the #V# is the bone named vomer, that the palatine bones are at its sides, and that its hinder parts are the pterygoid bones as in birds. There is a long, wide, four-sided, open space in the middle of the palate, between the vomer and the basi-sphenoid bone, unlike anything in birds or other animals.

Professor Marsh, in a figure of the palate in the great skull of the toothless

Pterodactyle named Ornithostoma (Pteranodon), from the Chalk of Kansas, found a large oval vacuity in this region of the palate. In that genus the pterygoid bones meet each other between the quadrate bones as in Dicynodon (Fig. 73, p. 182). Hence the great palatal vacuity here seen in the Ornithosaur is paralleled by the small vacuity in the South African reptile, which is sometimes distinct and sometimes partly separated from the anterior part of the vacuity which forms the openings of the nostrils on the palate.

The Solenhofen skulls which give any evidence of the palate are exposed in side view only, and the bones, imperfectly seen through the lateral vacuities, are displaced by crushing. They include long strips like the vomerine bones in the Lias fossil, and they diverge in the same way as they extend back to the quadrate bones. The oblique division into vomer in front and pterygoid bone behind is shown by Goldfuss in his original figure of Scaphognathus. Thus there is some reason for believing that all Ornithosaurs have the palate formed upon the same general plan, which is on the whole peculiar to the group, especially in not having the palatal openings of the nares divided in the middle line. It would appear probable that the short-tailed animals have the pterygoid bones meeting in the middle line and triangular; and that they are slender rods entirely separate from each other in the long-tailed genera.

THE TEETH

The teeth are all of pointed, elongated shape, without distinction into the kinds seen in most mammals and named incisors, canines, and grinders. They are organs for grasping, like the teeth of the fish-eating Crocodile of India, and are not unlike the simple teeth of some Porpoises. They are often implanted in oblique oval sockets with raised borders, usually at some distance apart from each other, and have the crown pointed, flattened more on the outer side than on the inner side, usually directed forward and curved inward. As in many extinct animals allied to existing reptiles, the teeth are reproduced by germs, which originate on the inner side of the root and grow till they gradually absorb the substance of the old tooth, forming a new one in its place. Frequently in Solenhofen genera, like Scaphognathus and Pterodactylus, the successional tooth is seen in the jaw on the hinder border of the tooth in use. There is some variation in the character of bluntness or sharpness of the crowns in the different genera, and in their size.

The name Dimorphodon, given to the animal from the Lias of Lyme Regis, expresses the fact that the teeth are of two kinds. In the front of the jaw three or four large long teeth are found in the intermaxillary bone on each side, as in some Plesiosaurs, while the teeth found further back in the maxillary bone are smaller, and directed more vertically downward. This difference is more marked in the lower jaw than in the upper jaw. In Rhamphorhynchus the teeth are all relatively long and large, and directed obliquely forward, but absent from the extremities of the beak, as in the German genus from the Lias named Dorygnathus, in which the bone of the lower jaw (which alone is known) terminates in a compressed spear. In Scaphognathus the teeth are few, more vertical, and do not extend backward so far as in Rhamphorhynchus, but are carried forward to the extremity of the blunt, deep jaw.

In the short-tailed Pterodactyles the teeth are smaller, shorter, wider at the base of the crown, closer together, and do not extend so far backward in the jaw. In Ornithocheirus two teeth always project forward from the front of the jaw. Ornithostoma is toothless.

SUPPOSED HORNY BEAK

Sometimes a horny covering has been suggested for the beak, like that seen in birds or turtles, but no such structure has been preserved, even in the Solenhofen Slate, in which such a structure would seem as likely to be preserved as a wing membrane, though there is one doubtful exception. There are marks of fine blood vessels on some of the jaws, indicating a tough covering to the bone. In Rhamphorhynchus the jaws appear to gape towards their extremities as though the interspace had originally been occupied by organic substance like a horny beak.

LOWER JAW

The lower jaw varies in relative length with the vertical or horizontal position of the quadrate bone in the skull. In Dimorphodon the jaw is as long as the skull; but in the genera from the Oolitic rocks the mandible is somewhat shorter, and in Ornithostoma the discrepancy reaches its maximum. The hinder part of the jaw is never prolonged backward much beyond the articulation, differing in this respect from Crocodiles and Plesiosaurs.

The depth of the jaw varies. It is slender in Pterodactylus, and is probably stronger relatively to the skull in Scaphognathus than in any other form. It fits between the teeth and bones of the alveolar border in the skull, in all the genera. In Dimorphodon its hinder border is partly covered by the descending edge of the malar process which these animals develop in common with some Dinosaurs, and some Anomodont reptiles, and many of the lower mammals. In this hinder region the lower jaw is sometimes perforated, in the same way as in Crocodiles. That condition is observed in Dimorphodon, but is not found in Pterodactylus. The lower jaw is always composite, being formed by several bones, as among reptiles and birds. The teeth are in the dentary bone or bones, and these bones are almost always blended as in most birds and Turtles, and not separate from each other as among Crocodiles, Lizards, and Serpents.

An interesting contour for the lower border of the jaw is seen in Ornithostoma, as made known in figures of American examples by Professors Marsh and Williston. It deepens as it extends backwards for two-thirds its length, stops at an angle, and then the depth diminishes to the articulation with the skull. This angle of the lower jaw is a characteristic feature of the jaws of Mammals. It is seen in the monotreme Echidna, and is characteristic of some Theriodont Reptiles from South Africa, which in many ways resemble Mammals. The character is not seen in the jaws of specimens from the Oolitic rocks, but is developed in the toothed Ornithocheirus from the Cambridge Greensand, and is absent from the jaws of existing reptiles and birds.

SUMMARY OF CHARACTERS OF THE HEAD

Taken as a whole, the head differs from other types of animals in a blending of characters which at the present day are found among Birds and Reptiles, with some structures which occur in extinct groups of animals with similar affinities, and perhaps a slight indication of features common to the lowest mammals. It is chiefly upon the head that the diverse views of earlier writers have been based. Cuvier was impressed with the reptilian aspect of the teeth; but in later times discoveries were made of Birds with teeth--Archaeopteryx, Ichthyornis, Hesperornis. The teeth are quite reptilian, being not unlike miniature teeth of Mosasaurus. If those birds had been found prior to the discovery of Pterodactyles, the teeth might have been regarded as a link with the more ancient birds, rather than a crucial difference between birds and reptiles.

All the specimens show a lateral temporal hole in the bones behind the eye, and this is found in no bird or mammal, and is typical of such reptiles as Hatteria. The quadrate bone may not be so decisive as Cuvier thought it to be, for its form is not unlike the quadrate of a bird, and different, so far as I have seen, from that of living reptiles. This region of the head is reptilian, and if it occurred in a bird the character would be as astonishing as was the discovery of teeth in extinct birds. These characters of the head are also found in fossil animals named Dinosaurs, in association with many resemblances to birds in their bones.

The palate might conceivably be derived from that of Hatteria by enlarging the small opening in the middle line in that reptile till it extended forward between the vomera; but it is more easily compared with a bird, which the animal resembles in its beak, and in the position of the nares. Excepting certain Lizards, all true existing Reptiles have the nostrils far forward and bordered by two premaxillary bones instead of one intermaxillary, as in Birds and Ornithosaurs. If nothing were known of the animal but its head bones, it would be placed between Reptiles and Birds.

CHAPTER IX

THE BACKBONE, OR VERTEBRAL COLUMN

The backbone is a more deep-seated part of the skeleton than the head. It is more protected by its position, and has less varied functions to perform. Therefore it varies less in distinctive character within the limits of each of the classes of vertebrate animals than either the head or limbs. It is divided into neck bones, the cervical vertebrae; back bones, the dorsal vertebrae; loin bones, the lumbar vertebrae; the sacrum, or sacral vertebrae, which support the hind limbs; and the tail. Of these parts the tail is the least important, though it reaches a length in existing reptiles which sometimes exceeds the whole of the remainder of the body, and includes hundreds of vertebrae. It attains its maximum among serpents and lizards. In frogs it is practically absent. In some of the higher mammals it is a rudiment, which does not extend beyond the soft parts of the body.

THE NECK

The neck is more liable to vary than the back, with the habit of life of the animal. And although mammals almost always preserve the same number of seven bones in the neck, the bones vary in length between the short condition of the porpoise, in which the neck is almost lost, and the long bones which form the neck of the Llama, though even these may be exceeded by some fossil reptiles like Tanystrophoeus. In many mammals the neck bones do not differ in length or size from those of the back. In others, like the Horse and Ox, they are much broader and larger.

There is the same sort of variation in the bones of the neck among birds, some being slender like the Heron, others broad like the Swan. But there is also a singular variation in number of vertebral bones in a bird's neck. At fewest there are nine, which equals the exceptionally large number found among mammals in the neck of one of the Sloths. Usually birds have ten to fifteen cervical vertebrae, and in the Swan there are twenty-three. Most of the neck bones of birds are relatively long, and the length of the neck is often greater than the remainder of the vertebral column.

Reptiles usually have short necks. The common Turtle has eight bones in the neck, ten in the back. The two regions are sharply defined by the dorsal shield. Their articular ends are sometimes cupped in front, in the neck, sometimes cupped behind, or convex at both ends, or even flattened, or the articulation may be made exceptionally by the neural arch alone. Nine is the largest number of neck bones in existing Lizards, and there are usually nine in Crocodiles; so that reptiles closely approach mammals in number of the neck bones. It is remarkable that the maximum number in a mammal and in living reptiles should coincide with the minimum number in birds. Therefore the number of cervical vertebrae as an attribute of Mammal, Bird, or Reptile, can only be important from its constancy.

German naturalists affirm on clear evidence that the Solenhofen Pterodactyles have seven cervical vertebrae. In many specimens there can be no doubt about the number, because the neck bones are easily distinguished from those of the back by their size; but the number is not always easy to count.

As in Birds, the first vertebra, or atlas, in Pterodactyles is extremely short, and is generally--if not always--blended with the much longer second vertebra, named the axis. The front of the atlas forms a small rounded cup to articulate with the rounded ball of the basioccipital bone at the back of the skull. The third and fourth vertebrae are longer, but the length visibly shortens in the sixth and seventh.

Sometimes the vertebrae are slender and devoid of strong spinous processes. This is the condition in the little Pterodactylus longirostris and in the comparatively large Cycnorhamphus Fraasii, in which there is a slight median ridge along the upper surface of the arch of the vertebra. This condition is paralleled in birds with long necks, especially wading birds such as the Heron. Other Ornithosaurs, such as Ornithocheirus from the Cretaceous rocks, have the neck much more massive. The vertebrae are flattened on the under side. The arch above the nervous matter of the spinal cord has a more or less considerable transverse expansion, and may even be as wide as long. These vertebrae have proportions and form such as may be seen in Vultures or in the Swan. In either case the form of the neck bones is more or less bird-like, and the neural spine may be elevated, especially in Pterodactyles with long tails.

One of the most distinctive features of the neck bones of a bird is the way in which the cervical ribs are blended with the vertebrae. They are small, and each is often prolonged in a needle-like rod at the side of the neck bone.

In Ornithocheirus the cervical rib similarly blends with the vertebra by two articulations, as in mammals, so that it might escape notice but for the channel of a blood vessel which is thus inclosed. In several of the older Pterodactyles from Solenhofen the ribs of the neck vertebrae remain separated, as in a Crocodile, though still bird-like in their form, anterior position, and mode of attachment. In Terrapins and Tortoises the long neck vertebrae have no cervical ribs.

The articular surfaces between the bodies of the vertebrae, in the neck, are transversely oval. The middle part of this articular joint is made by the body of the vertebra; its outer parts are in the neural arch. In front this surface is a hollow channel, often more depressed than in any other animals. The corresponding surface behind is convex, with a process on each side at its lower outer angles (Fig. 25). It is a modification of the cup-and-ball form of vertebral articulation, which at the present day is eminently reptilian. Serpents and Crocodiles have the articulations similarly vertical, but in both the form of the articulation is a circle. In Lizards the articular cup is usually rather wider than deep, when the cup and ball are developed in the vertebrae; it differs from the vertical condition in pterodactyles in being oblique and much narrower from side to side. Only among Crocodiles and Hatteria is there a double articulation for the cervical rib, though in neither order have rib or vertebra in the neck the bird-like proportions which are usual in these animals. Pterodactyles show no resemblance to birds in this vertebral articulation. A Bird has the corresponding surface concave from side to side in front, but it is also convex from above downward, producing what is known as the saddle-shaped form which is peculiarly avian, being found in existing birds except in part of the back in Penguins. It is faintly approximated to in one or two neck vertebrae in man. Professor Williston remarks that in the toothless Pterodactyles of Kansas the hinder ball of the vertebral articulation is continued downward and outward as a concave articulation upon the processes at its outer corners. There are no mammals with a cup-and-ball articulation between the vertebrae, so that for what it is worth the character now described in Ornithosaurs is reptilian, when judged by comparison with existing animals.

Low down on each side of the vertebra, at the junction of its body with the neural arch, is a large ovate foramen, transversely elongated, and often a little impressed at the border, which is the entrance of the air cell into the bone. These foramina are often one-third of the length of the neck vertebrae in specimens from the Cambridge Greensand, where the neck bones vary from three-quarters of an inch to about two and a half inches in length, and in extreme forms are as wide as long. The width of the interspace between the foramina is one-half the width of the vertebrae, though this character varies with different genera and species. Several species from the Solenhofen Slate have the neck long and slender, on the type of the Flamingo. In others the neck is thick and short--in the Scaphognathus crassirostris and Pterodactylus spectabilis. Some genera with slender necks have the bones preserved with a curved contour, such as might suggest a neck carried like that of a Llama or a Camel. The neck is occasionally preserved in a curve like a capital #S#, as though about to be darted forward like that of a bird in the act of striking its prey. The genera of Pterodactyles with short necks may have had as great mobility of neck as is found among birds named Ducks and Divers; but those Pterodactyles with stout necks, such as Dimorphodon and Ornithocheirus, in which the vertebrae are large, appear to have been built more for strength than activity, and the neck bones have been chiefly concerned in the muscular effort to use the fighting power of the jaws in the best way.

THE BACK

The region of the back in a Pterodactyle is short as compared with the neck, and relatively is never longer than the corresponding region in a bird. The shortness results partly from the short length of the vertebrae, each of which is about as long as wide. There is also a moderate number of bones in the back. In most skeletons from Solenhofen these vertebrae between the neck and girdle of hip bones number from twelve to sixteen. They have a general resemblance in form to the dorsal vertebrae in birds. The greatest number of such vertebrae in birds is eleven. The number is small because some of the later vertebrae in birds are overlapped by the bones of the hip girdle, which extend forward and cover them at the sides, so that they become blended with the sacrum. This region of the skeleton in the Dimorphodon from the Lias is remarkable for the length of the median process, named the neural spine, which is prolonged upward like the spines of the early dorsal vertebrae of Horses, Deer, and other mammals. In this character they differ from living reptiles, and parallel some Dinosaurs from the Weald. The bones of the back in Ornithocheirus from the Cambridge Greensand show the under side to be well rounded, so that the articular surfaces between the vertebrae, though still rather wider than deep, are much less depressed than in the region of the neck. The neural canal for the spinal cord has become larger and higher, and the sides of the bone are somewhat compressed. Strong transverse processes for the support of the ribs are elevated above the level of the neural canal, at the sides of vertebrae compressed on the under sides, and directed outward. Between these lateral horizontal platforms is the compressed median neural spine, which varies in vertical height. The articulation of the ribs is not seen clearly. Isolated ribs from the Stonesfield Slate have double-headed dorsal ribs, like those of birds. In some specimens from the Solenhofen Slate like the

Scaphognathus, in the University Museum at Bonn, dorsal ribs appear to be attached by a notch in the transverse process of the dorsal vertebra, which resembles the condition in Crocodiles. Variations in the mode of attachment of ribs among mammals may show that character to be of subordinate importance. Von Meyer has described the first pair of ribs as frequently larger than the others, and there appear in Rhamphorhynchus to be examples preserved of the sternal ribs, which connect the dorsal ribs with the sternum. Six pairs have been counted. A more interesting feature in the ribs consists in the presence behind the sternum, which is shorter than the corresponding bone in most birds, of median sternal ribs. They are slender #V#-shaped bones in the middle line of the abdomen, which overlapped the ends of the dorsal ribs like the similar sternal bones of reptiles. Such structures are unknown among Birds and Mammals. There is no trace in the dorsal ribs of the claw-like process, which extends laterally from rib to rib as a marked feature in many birds. Its presence or absence may not be important, because it is represented by fibro-cartilage in the ribs of crocodiles, and may be a small cartilage near the head of the rib in serpents, and is only ossified in some ribs of the New Zealand reptile Hatteria. So that it might have been present in a fossil animal without being ossified and preserved. Although the structure is associated with birds, it is possibly also represented by the great bony plates which cover the ribs in Chelonians, and combine to form the shield which covers the turtle's back. The structure is as characteristic of reptiles as of birds, but is not necessarily associated with either.

There are two remarkable modifications of the early dorsal vertebrae in some of the Cretaceous Pterodactyles. First, in the genus Ornithodesmus from the Weald the early dorsal vertebrae are blended together into a continuous mass, like that which is found in the corresponding region of the living Frigate-bird, only more consolidated, and similar to that consolidated structure found behind the dorsal vertebrae, known as the sacrum, made by the blending of the vertebrae into a solid mass which supports the hip bones. Secondly, in some of the Cretaceous genera of Pterodactyles of Europe and America the vertebrae in the front part of the back are similarly blended, but their union is less complete; and in genera Ornithocheirus and Ornithostoma- -the former chiefly English, the latter chiefly American--the sides of the neural spines are flattened to form an oval articular surface on each side, which gives attachment to the flattened ends of their shoulder-blade bones named the scapulae. This condition is found in no other animals. Three vertebrae appear to have their neural arches thus united together. The structure so formed may be named the notarium to distinguish it from the sacrum.

SACRUM

For some mysterious reason the part of the backbone which lies between the bones of the hips and supports them is termed the sacrum. Among living reptiles the number of vertebrae in this region is usually two, as in lizards and crocodiles. There are other groups of fossil reptiles in which the number of sacral vertebrae is in some cases less and in other cases more. There is, perhaps, no group in which the sacrum makes a nearer approach to that of birds than is found among these Pterodactyles, although there are more sacral vertebrae in some Dinosaurs. In birds the sacral vertebrae number from five to twenty-two. In bats the number is from five to six. In some Solenhofen species, such as Pterodactylus dubius and P. Kochi and P. grandipelvis, the number is usually five or six. The vertebrae are completely blended. The pneumatic foramina in the sacrum, so far as they have been observed, are on the under sides of the transverse processes; while in the corresponding notarial structure in the shoulder girdle the foramina are in front of the transverse processes. Almost any placental mammal in which the vertebrae of the sacral region are anchylosed together has a similar sacrum, which differs from that of birds in the more complete individuality of the constituent bones remaining evident. The transverse processes in front of the sacrum are wider than in its hinder part; so that the pelvic bones which are attached to it converge as they extend backward, as among mammals. The bodies of the vertebrae forming the sacrum are similar in length to those of the back. Each transverse process is given off opposite the body of its own vertebra, but from a lower lateral position than in the region of the back, in which the vertebrae are free.

The hip bones are closely united with the sacrum by bony union, and rarely appear to come away from the sacral vertebrae, as among mammals and reptiles, though this happens with the Lias Pterodactyles. In the Stonesfield Slate and Solenhofen Slate the slender transverse processes from the vertebrae blend with the ilium of the hip girdle, and form a series of transverse foramina on each side of the bodies of the vertebrae. In the Cambridge Greensand genera the part of the ilium above the acetabulum for the articular head of the femur appears to be always broken away, so that the relation of the sacrum to the pelvis has not been observed. This character is no mark of affinity, but only shows that ossification obliterated sutures among these animals in the same way as among birds.

The great difference between the sacrum of a Pterodactyle and that of a bird has been rendered intelligible by the excellent discussion of the sacral region in birds made by Professor Huxley. He showed that it is only the middle part of the sacrum of a chicken which corresponds to the true sacrum of a reptile, and comprises the five shortest of the vertebrae; while the four in front correspond to those of the lower part of the back, which either bear no ribs or very short ribs, and are known as the lumbar region in mammals, so that the lower part of the back becomes blended with the sacrum, and thus reduces the number of dorsal vertebrae. Similarly the five vertebrae which follow the true sacral vertebrae are originally part of the tail, and have been blended with the other vertebrae in front, in consequence of the extension along them of the bird's hip bones. This interpretation helps to account for the great length of the sacrum in many birds, and also explains in part the singular shortness of the tail in existing birds. The Ornithosaur sacrum has neither the lumbar nor the caudal portions of the sacrum of a bird.

THE TAIL

The tail is perhaps the least important part of the skeleton, since it varies in character and length in different genera. The short tails seen in typical pterodactyles include as few as ten vertebrae in Pterodactylus grandipelvis and P. Kochi, and as many as fifteen vertebrae in Pterodactylus longirostris. The tails are more like those of mammals than existing birds, in which there are usually from six to ten vertebrae terminating in the ploughshare bone. But just as some fossil birds, like the Archaeopteryx, have about twenty long and slender vertebrae in the tail, so in the pterodactyle Rhamphorhynchus this region becomes greatly extended, and includes from thirty-eight to forty vertebrae. In Dimorphodon the tail vertebrae are slightly fewer. The earliest are very short, and then they become elongated to two or three times the length of the early tail vertebrae, and finally shorten again towards the extremity of the tail, where the bones are very slender. In all long-tailed Ornithosaurians the vertebrae are supported and bordered by slender ossified ligaments, which extend like threads down the tail, just as they do in Rats and many other mammals and in some lizards.

Professor Marsh was able to show that the extremity of the tail in Rhamphorhynchus sometimes expands into a strong terminal caudal membrane of four-sided somewhat rhomboidal shape. He regards this membrane as having been placed vertically. It is supported by delicate processes which represent the neural spines of the vertebrae prolonged upward. They are about fifteen in number. A corresponding series of spines on the lower border, termed chevron bones, equally long, were given off from the junctions of the vertebrae on their under sides, and produced downward. This vertical appendage is of some interest because its expansion is like the tail of a fish. It suggests the possibility of having been used in a similar way to the caudal fin as an organ for locomotion in water, though it is possible that it may have also formed an organ used in flight for steering in the air.

The tail vertebrae from the Cambridge Greensand are mostly found isolated or with not more than four joints in association. They are very like the slender type of neck vertebrae seen in long-necked pterodactyles, but are depressed, and though somewhat wider are not unlike the tail vertebrae of the Rhamphorhynchus. The pneumatic foramen in them is a mere puncture. They have no transverse processes or neural spines, nor indications of ribs, or chevron bones.

The hindermost specimens of tail vertebrae observed have the neural arch preserved to the end, as among reptiles; whereas in mammals this arch becomes lost towards the end of the tail. The processes by which the vertebrae are yoked together are small. There is nothing to suggest that the tail was long, except the circumstance that the slender caudal vertebrae are almost as long as the stout cervical vertebrae in the same animal. No small caudal vertebrae have ever been found in the Cambridge Greensand. The tail is very short, according to Professor Williston, in the toothless Ornithostoma in the Chalk of Kansas.

CHAPTER X

THE HIP-GIRDLE AND HIND LIMB

The bones of the hip-girdle form a basin which incloses and protects the abdominal vital organs. It consists on each side of a composite bone, the unnamed bones--ossa innominata of the older anatomists--which are each attached to the sacrum on their inner side, and on the outer side give attachment to the hind limbs. As a rule three bones enter into the borders of this cup, termed the acetabulum, in which the head of the thigh bone, named the Femur, moves with a more or less rotary motion.

There are a few exceptions in this division of the cup between three bones, chiefly among Salamanders and certain Frogs. In Crocodiles the bone below the acetabular cup is not divided into two parts. And in certain Plesiosaurs from the Oxford Clay--Muraenosaurus--the actual articulation appears to be made by two bones--the ilium and ischium. The three bones which form each side of the pelvis are known as the ilium, or hip bone, sometimes termed the aitch bone; secondly, the ischium, or sitz bone, being the bone by which the body is supported in a sitting position; and thirdly the pubis, which is the bone in front of the acetabulum. The pubic bones meet in the middle line of the body on the under side of the pelvis in man, and on each side are partly separated from the ischia by a foramen, spoken of as the obturator foramen, which in Pterodactyles is minute and almost invisible, when it exists.

There is often a fourth bony element in the pelvis. In some Salamanders a single cartilage is directed forward, and forked in front. According to Professor Huxley something of this kind is seen in the Dog. The pair of bones which extend forward in front of the pelvis in Crocodiles may be of the same kind, in which case they should be called prepubic bones. But among the lower mammals named marsupials a pouch is developed for the protection of the young and supported by two slender bones attached to the pubes, and these bones have long been known as marsupial bones. In a still lower group of mammalia named monotremata, which lay eggs, and in many ways approximate to reptiles and birds, stronger bones are developed on the front edge of the pubes, and termed prepubic bones. They do not support a marsupium.

Naturalists have been uncertain as to the number of bones in the pelvis of Pterodactyles, because the bones blend together early in life, as in birds. Some follow the Amphibian nomenclature, and unite the ischium and pubis into one bone, which is then termed ischium, when the prepubis is termed the pubis, and regarded as removed from the acetabulum. There is no ground for this interpretation, for the sutures are clear between the three pelvic bones in the acetabulum in some specimens, like Cycnorhamphus Fraasii, from Solenhofen, and some examples of Ornithocheirus from the Cambridge Greensand. Pterodactyles all have prepubic bones, which are only known in Ornithorhynchus and Echidna among mammals, and are absent from the higher mammals and birds. They are unknown in any other existing animals, unless present in Crocodiles, in which ischium and pubis are always undivided. Therefore it is interesting to examine the characters of the Ornithosaurian pelvis.

The acetabulum for the head of the femur is imperforate, being a simple oval basin, as in Chelonian reptiles and the higher Mammals. It never shows the mark of the ligamentous attachment to the head of the femur, which is seen in Mammals. In Birds the acetabulum is perforated, as in many of the fossils named Dinosaurs, and in Monotremata.

Secondly, the ilium is elongated, and extends quite as much in front of the acetabulum as behind it. The bone is not very deep in this front process. Among existing animals this relation of the bone is nearer to birds than to any other type, since birds alone have the ilium extended from the acetabulum in both directions. The form of the Pterodactyle ilium is usually that of the embryo bird, and its slender processes compare in relative length better with those of the unhatched fowl and Apteryx of New Zealand than with the plate-like form in adult birds.

In mammals the ilium is directed forward, and even in the Cape ant-eater Orycteropus there is only an inappreciable production of the bone backward behind the acetabulum. Among reptiles the general position of the acetabulum is at the forward termination of the ilium, though the Crocodile has some extension of the bone in both directions, without forming distinct anterior and posterior processes. This anterior and posterior extension of the ilium is seen in the Theriodont reptiles of Russia and of South Africa, as well as in Dinosaurs.

Thirdly, in all pterodactyles the ischium and pubis are more or less completely blended into a sheet of bone, unbroken by perforation, though there is usually a minute vascular foramen; or the lower border may be notched between the ischium and the pubis, as in some of the Solenhofen species, and the pubis does not reach the median line of the body. But in Dimorphodon the pelvic sheet of bone is unbroken by any notch or perforation. The notch between the ischium and pubis is well marked in Pterodactylus longirostris, and better marked in Pterodactylus dubius, Cycnorhamphus Fraasii, and Rhamphorhynchus. The fossil animals which appear to come nearest to the Pterodactyles in the structure of the pelvis are Theriodonts from the Permian rocks of Russia. The type known as Rhopalodon has the ilium less prolonged front and back, and is much deeper than in any Pterodactyle; but the acetabulum is imperforate, and the ischium and pubis are not always completely separated from each other by suture. In the pelvis referred to the Theriodont Deuterosaurus there is some approximation to the pelvis of Rhamphorhynchus and of Pterodactylus dubius in the depth of the division between the pubis and ischium.

There are three modifications of the Ornithosaurian pelvis. First, the type of Rhamphorhynchus, in which the pubis and ischium are inclined somewhat backward, and in which the two prepubic bones are triangular, and are often united together to form a transverse bow in front of the pubic region.

Secondly, there is the ordinary form of pelvis in which the pubis and ischium usually unite with each other down their length, as in Dimorphodon, but sometimes, as in Pterodactylus dubius, divide immediately below the acetabulum. All these types possess the paddle-shaped prepubic bones, which are never united in the median line.

Thirdly, there is the cretaceous form indicated by Ornithocheirus and Ornithostoma, in which the posterior half of the ilium is modified in a singular way, since it is more elevated towards the sacrum than the anterior half, suggesting the contour of the upper border of the ilium in a lizard. Without being reptilian--the anterior prolongation of the bone makes that impossible--it suggests the lizards. This type also possesses prepubic bones. They appear, according to Professor Williston, to be more like the paddle-shaped bones of Pterodactylus than like the angular bones in Rhamphorhynchus. The prepubic bones are united in the median line as in Rhamphorhynchus. But their median union in that genus favours the conclusion that the bones were united in the median line in all species, though they are only co-ossified in these two families.

This median union of the prepubic bones is a difference from those mammals like the Ornithorhynchus and Echidna, which approach nearest to the Reptilia. In them the prepubic bones have a long attachment to the front margin of the pubis, and extend their points forward without any tendency for the anterior extremities to approximate or unite. The marsupial mammals have the same character, keeping the marsupial bones completely distinct from each other at their free extremities. The only existing animals in which an approximation is found to the prepubic bones in Pterodactyles are Crocodiles, in bones which most writers term the pubic bones. This resemblance, without showing any strong affinity with the Crocodilia, indicates that Crocodiles have more in common with the fossil flying animals than any other group of existing reptiles; for other reptiles all want prepubic bones, or bones in front of the pubic region.

THE HIND LIMB

The hind limb is exceptionally long in proportion to the back. This is conspicuous in the skeletons of the short-tailed Pterodactyles, and is also seen in Dimorphodon. In Rhamphorhynchus the hind limb is relatively much shorter, so that the animal, when on all fours, may have had an appearance not unlike a Bat in similar position. The limb is exceptionally short in the little Ptenodracon brevirostris. The bones of the hind limb are exceptionally interesting. One remarkable feature common to all the specimens is the great elongation of the shin bones relatively to the thigh bones. The femur is sometimes little more than half the length of the tibia, and always shorter than that bone. The proportions are those of mammals and birds. Some mammals have the leg shorter than the thigh, but mammals and birds alone, among existing animals, have the proportions which characterise Pterodactyles. The foot appears to have been applied to the ground not always as in a bird, but more often in the manner of reptiles, or mammals in which the digits terminate in claws.

THE FEMUR

The thigh bone, on account of the small size of many of the specimens, is not always quite clear evidence as an indication of technical resemblance to other animals. The bone is always a little curved, has always a rounded, articular head, and rounded distal condyles. Its most remarkable features are shown in the large, well-preserved specimens from the Cambridge Greensand. The rounded, articular head is associated with a constricted neck to the bone, followed by a comparatively straight shaft with distal condyles, less thickened than in mammals. No bird is known, much less any reptile, with a femur like Ornithocheirus. Only among Mammals is a similar bone known with a distinct neck; and only a few mammals have the exceptional characters of the rounded head and constricted neck at all similar to the Cretaceous Pterodactyles. A few types, such as the higher apes, the Hyrax, and animals especially active in the hind limb, have a femur at all resembling the Pterodactyle in the pit for the obturator externus muscle, behind the trochanter major, such as is seen in a small femur from Ashwell. The femur varies in different genera, so as to suggest a number of mammalia rather than any particular animal for comparison. These approximations may be consequences of the ways in which the bones are used. When functional modifications of the skeleton are developed, so as to produce similar forms of bones, the muscles to which they give attachment, which act upon the bones, and determine their growth, are substantially the same. In the Pterodactylus longirostris the femur corresponds in length to about eleven dorsal vertebrae. The end next the shin bone is less expanded than is usual among Mammals, and rather suggests an approach to the condition in Crocodiles, in the moderate thickness and breadth of the articular end, and the slight development of the terminal pulley-joint. One striking feature of the femur is the circumstance that the articular head, as compared with the distal end, is directed forward and very slightly inward and upward. So that allowing for the outward divergence of the pelvic bones, as they extend forward, there must have been a tendency to a knock-kneed approximation of the lower ends of the thigh bones, as in Mammals and Birds, rather than the outward divergence seen in Reptiles.

Apparently the swing of the leg and foot, as it hung on the distal end of the femur, must have tended rather to an inward than to an outward direction, so that the feet might be put down upon the same straight line; this arrangement suggests rapid movement.

TIBIA AND FIBULA

In Pterodactylus longirostris the tibia is slender, more than a fifth longer than the femur. A crest is never developed at the proximal end, like that seen in the Guillemot and Diver and other water birds. The bone is of comparatively uniform thickness down the shaft in most of the Solenhofen specimens, as in most birds. At the distal end the shin bone commonly has a rounded, articular termination, like that seen in birds. This is conspicuous in the Pterodactylus grandis. In other specimens the tarsal bones, which form this pulley, remain distinct from the tibia; and the upper row of these bones appears to consist of two bones, like those which in many Dinosaurs combine to form the pulley-like end of the tibia which represents the bird's drum-stick bone. They correspond with the ankle bones in man named astragalus and os calcis.

Complete English specimens of tibia and fibula are found in the genus Dimorphodon from the Lias, in which the terminal pulley of the distal end has some expansion, and is placed forward towards the front of the tibia, as in some birds. The rounded surface of the pulley is rather better marked than in birds. The proximal end of the shaft is relatively stout, and is modified by the well-developed fibula, which is a short external splint bone limited to the upper half of the tibia, as in birds; but contributing with it to form the articular surface for the support of the lower end of the femur, taking a larger share in that work than in birds. Frequently there is no trace of the fibula visible in Solenhofen specimens as preserved; or it is extremely slender and bird-like, as in Pterodactylus longirostris. In Rhamphorhynchus it appears to extend the entire length of the tibia, as in Dinosaurs. In the specimens from the Cambridge Greensand there is indication of a small proximal crest to the tibia with a slight ridge, but no evidence that this is due to a separate ossification. The patella, or knee-cap, is not recognised in any fossil of the group. There is no indication of a fibula in the specimens thus far known from the Chalk rocks either of Kansas in America, or in England.

The region of the tarsus varies from the circumstance that in many specimens the tibia terminates downward in a rounded pulley, like the drum-stick of a bird; while in other specimens this union of the proximal row of the tarsal bones with the tibia does not take place, and then there are two rows of separate tarsal bones, usually with two bones in each row. When the upper row is united with the tibia the lower row remains distinct from the metatarsus, though no one has examined these separate tarsal bones so as to define them.

THE FOOT

The foot sometimes has four toes, and sometimes five. There are four somewhat elongated, slender metatarsal bones, which are separate from each other and never blended together, as in birds. There has been a suspicion that the metatarsal bones were separate in the young Archaeopteryx. In the young of many birds the row of tarsal bones at the proximal end of the metatarsus comes away, and there is a partial division between the metatarsal bones, though they remain united in the middle. And among Penguins, in which the foot bones are applied to the ground instead of being carried in the erect position of ordinary birds, there is always a partial separation between the metatarsal bones, though they become blended together. The Pterodactyle is therefore different from birds in preserving the bones distinct through life, and this character is more like Reptiles than Mammals. The individual bones are not like those of Dinosaurs, and diverge in Rhamphorhynchus as though the animals were web-footed. There is commonly a rudimentary fifth metatarsal. It is sometimes only a claw-shaped appendage, like that seen in the Crocodile. It is sometimes a short bone, completely formed, and carrying two phalanges in Solenhofen specimens: though no trace of these phalanges is seen in the large toothless Pterodactyles from the Cretaceous rocks of North America. In the Pterodactylus longirostris the number of foot bones on the ordinary digits is two, three, four, five, as in lizards; but the short fifth metatarsal has only two toe bones. In Dimorphodon the fifth digit was bent upward, and supported a membrane for flight. There are slight variations in the number of foot bones. In the species Pterodactylus scolopaciceps the number of bones in the toes follows the formula two, three, three, four. In Pterodactylus micronyx the number is two, three, three, three. The terminal claws are much less developed than is usual with Birds; and there is a difference from Bats in the unequal length of the digits. Taken as a whole, the foot is perhaps more reptilian than avian, and in some genera is crocodilian.

The foot is the light foot of an active animal. Von Meyer thought that the hind legs were too slender to enable the animal to walk on land; and Professor Williston, of the University of Kansas, remarks that the rudimentary claws and weak toes indicate that the animal could not have used the feet effectively for grasping, while the exceedingly free movement of the femur indicates great freedom of movement of the hind legs; and he concludes that the function of the legs was chiefly for guidance in flight through their control over the movements, and expresses his belief that the animal could not have stood upon the ground with its feet. There may be evidence to sustain other views. If the limb bones are reconstructed, they form limbs not wanting in elegance or length. If it is true, as Professor Williston suggests, that the weight of his largest animals with the head three feet long, and a stretch of wing of eighteen or nineteen feet, did not exceed twenty pounds, there can be no objection to regarding these animals as quadrupeds, or even as bipeds, on the ground of the limbs lacking the strength necessary to support the body. The slender toes of many birds, and even the two toes of the ostrich, may be thought to give less adequate support for those animals than the metatarsals and digits of Pterodactyles.

CHAPTER XI

SHOULDER-GIRDLE AND FORE LIMB

STERNUM

The sternum is always a distinguishing part of the bony structure of the breast. In Crocodiles it is a cartilage to which the sternal ribs unite; and upon its front portion a flat knife-like bone called the interclavicle is placed. In lizards like the Chameleon, it is a lozenge-shaped structure of thin bony texture, also bearing a long interclavicle, which supports the clavicular bones, named collar bones in man, which extend outward to the shoulder blades. Among mammals the sternum is usually narrow and flat, and often consists of many successive pieces in the middle line, on the under side of the body. Among Bats the anterior part is somewhat widened from side to side, to give attachment to the collar bones, but the sternum still remains a narrow bone, much narrower than in Dolphins, and not differing in character from many other Mammals, notwithstanding the Bat's power of flight. The bone develops a median keel for the attachment of the muscles of the breast, but something similar is seen in burrowing Insectivorous mammals like the Moles. So that, as Von Meyer remarked, the presence of a keel on the sternum is not in itself sufficient evidence to prove flight.

Among birds the sternum is greatly developed. Broad and short in the Ostrich tribe, it is devoid of a keel; and therefore the keel, if present in a bird, is suggestive of flight. The keel is differently developed according to the mode of attachment of the several pectoral muscles which cover a bird's breast. In several water birds the keel is strongly developed in front, and dies away towards the hinder part of the sternum, as in the Cormorant and its allies. The sternum in German Pterodactyles is most nearly comparable to these birds.

In the Solenhofen Slate the sternum is fairly well preserved in many Ornithosaurs. It is relatively shorter than in birds, and is broader than long; but not very like the sternum of reptile or mammal in form. The keel is limited to the anterior part of the shield of the sternum, as in Merganser and the Cormorant, and is prolonged forward for some distance in advance of it. Von Meyer noticed the resemblance of this anterior process to the interclavicle of the Crocodile in position; but it is more like the keel of a bird's sternum, and is not a separate bone as in Reptiles. In Pterodactyles from the Cretaceous rocks, the side bones, called coracoids, are articulated to saddle-shaped surfaces at the hinder part of the base of this keel, which are parallel in Ornithocheirus, as in most birds, but overlap in Ornithodesmus, as in Herons and wading birds.

The keel was pneumatic, and when broken is seen to be hollow, and appears to have been exceptionally high in Rhamphorhynchus, a genus in which the wing bones are greatly elongated. Von Meyer found in Rhamphorhynchus on each side of the sternum a separate lateral plate with six pairs of sternal ribs, which unite the sternum with the dorsal ribs, as in the young of some birds. The hinder surface of the sternum is imperfectly preserved in the toothless Pterodactyles of Kansas. Professor Williston states that the bone is extremely thin and pentagonal in outline, projecting in front of the coracoids, in a stout, blunt, keel-like process, similar to that seen in the Pterodactyles of the Cambridge Greensand. American specimens have not the same notch behind the articulation for the coracoid to separate it from the transverse lateral expansion of the sternal shield. The lateral margin in the Cambridge Greensand specimens figured by Professor Owen and myself is broken; but Professor Williston had the good fortune to find on the margin of the sternum the articular surfaces which gave attachment to the sternal ribs. The margin of the sternal bone thickens at these facets, four of which are preserved. The sternum in Ornithostoma was about four and a half inches long by less than five and a half inches wide. The median keel extends forward for rather less than two inches, while in the smaller Cambridge species of Ornithocheirus it extends forward for less than an inch and a half.

A sternum of this kind is unlike that of any other animal, but has most in common with a bird; and may be regarded as indicating considerable power of flight. The bone cannot be entirely attributed to the effect of flight, since there is no such expanded sternal shield in Bats. The small number of sternal ribs is even more characteristic of birds than mammals or reptiles.

THE SHOULDER-GIRDLE

The bones which support the fore limb are one of the distinctive regions of the skeleton defining the animal's place in nature. Among most of the lower vertebrata, such as Amphibians and Reptiles, the girdle is a double arch--the arch of the collar bone or clavicles in front, and the arch of the shoulder-blade or scapula behind. The clavicular arch, when it exists, is formed of three or five parts--a medium bar named the interclavicle, external to which is a pair of bones called clavicles, reaching to the front of the scapulae when they are present; and occasionally there is a second pair of bones called supraclavicles, extending from the clavicles up the front margins of the scapulae. Thus the clavicular arch is placed in front of the scapular arch. The supraclavicles are absent from all living Reptiles, and the clavicles are absent from Crocodiles. The interclavicle is absent from all mammals except Echidna and Ornithorhynchus. Clavicles also may be absent in some orders of mammals. Hence the clavicular arch may be lost, though the collar bones are retained in man.

The scapular arch also is more complicated and more important in the lower than in the higher vertebrata. It may include three bones on each side named coracoid, precoracoid, and scapula. But in most vertebrates the coracoid and precoracoid appear never to have been segmented so as to be separated from each other; and it is only among extinct types of reptiles, which appear to approximate to the Monotreme mammals, that separate precoracoid bones are found; though among most mammals, probably, there are stages of early development in which precoracoids are represented by small cartilages, though few mammals except Edentata like the Sloths and Ant-eaters, retain even the coracoids as distinct bones. Therefore, excepting the Edentata and the Monotremes, the distinctive feature of the mammalian shoulder-girdle appears to be that the limbs are supported by the shoulder-blades, termed the scapulae.

Among reptiles there are several distinct types of shoulder-girdle. Chelonians possess a pair of bones termed coracoids which have no connexion with a sternum; and their scapulae are formed of two widely divergent bars, divided by a deeper notch than is found in any fossil reptiles. Among Lizards both scapula and coracoid are widely expanded, and the coracoid is always attached to the sternum. Chameleons have the blade of the scapula long and slender, but the coracoid is always as broad as it is long. Crocodiles have the bone more elongated, so that it has somewhat the aspect of a very strong first sternal rib when seen on the ventral face of the animal. The bone is perforated by a foramen, which would probably lie in the line of separation from the precoracoid if any such separation had ever taken place. The scapula, or shoulder-blade, of Crocodiles is a similar flat bone, very much shorter than the scapula of a Chameleon, and more like that of the New Zealand Hatteria. Thus there is very little in common between the several reptilian types of shoulder-girdle.

In birds the apparatus for the support of the wings has a far-off resemblance to the Crocodilian type. The coracoid bones, instead of being directed laterally outward and upward from the sternum, as among Crocodiles, are directed forward, so as to prolong the line of the breast bone, named the sternum. The bird's coracoid is sometimes flattened towards the breast bone among Swans and other birds; yet as a rule the coracoid is a slender bar, which combines with the still more slender and delicate blade of the scapula, which rests on the ribs, to make the articulation for the upper arm bone. Among reptiles the scapula and coracoid are more or less in the same straight line, as in the Ostrich, but in birds of flight they meet at an angle which is less than a right angle, and where they come in contact the external surface is thickened and excavated to make the articulation for the head of the humerus. There is nothing like this shoulder-girdle outside the class of birds, until it is compared with the corresponding structure in these extinct animals called Pterodactyles. The resemblance between the two is surprising. It is not merely the identity of form in the coracoid bone and the scapula, but the similar angle at which they meet and the similar position of the articulation for the humerus. Everything in the Pterodactyle's shoulder-girdle is bird-like, except the absence of the representative of the clavicles, that forked #V#-

shaped bone of the bird which in scientific language is known as the furculum, and is popularly termed the "merry-thought." This kind of shoulder-girdle is found in the genera from the Lias and the Oolitic rocks, both of this country and Germany.

In the Cretaceous rocks the scapula presents, in most cases, a different appearance. The coracoid is an elongated, somewhat triangular bone, compressed on the outer margin as in birds, but differing alike from birds and other Pterodactyles in not being prolonged forward beyond the articulation for the humerus. In these Cretaceous genera, toothed and toothless alike, the articulation for the upper arm bone truncates the extremity of the coracoid, so that the bone is less like that of a bird in this feature. Perhaps it shows a modification towards the crocodilian direction. The scapula, which unites with the coracoid at about a right angle, is similarly truncated by the articular surface for the humerus; but the bone is somewhat expanded immediately beyond the articulation, and compressed; and instead of being directed backward, it is directed inward over the ribs to articulate with the neural arches of the early dorsal vertebrae in the genera found in strata associated with the Chalk. As the bone approaches this articulation, it thickens and widens a little, becoming suddenly truncated by an ovate facet, which exactly corresponds to the transversely ovate impression, concave from front to back, which is seen in the neural arches of the dorsal vertebrae on which it fits. This condition is not present in all Cretaceous Pterodactyles. It does not occur in the Kansas fossil, named by Professor Marsh, Nyctodactylus. And it appears to be absent from the Pterodactyles of the English Weald, named Ornithodesmus.

There is no approach to this transverse position of the scapulae among birds. And while the form of the bones in the older genera of Ornithosaurs is singularly bird-like, the angular arrangement in this Cretaceous genus is obtained by closely approximating the articulations on the sternum, so that the coracoids extend outward as in reptiles, instead of forward as in birds; and the extremities of the scapulae similarly approximate towards each other. This rather recalls the relative positions of scapula and coracoid among crocodiles. If crocodile and bird had been primitive types of animals instead of surviving types, it might almost seem as though there had been a cunning and harmonious blending of one with the other in evolving this form of shoulder-girdle.

THE FORE LIMB

The bones of the fore limb, generally, correspond in length with the similar parts of the hind limb. The upper arm bone corresponds with the upper leg bone, and the fore-arm bone is as long as the fore-leg bone; then differences begin. The bones which correspond to the back of the hand in man, termed the metacarpus, are variable in length in Pterodactyles--sometimes very long and sometimes short. The wing metacarpal bone is always stout, and the others are slender. The extremity of the metacarpus was applied to the ground. Three small digits of the hand are developed from the three small metacarpal bones, and terminate in large claws.

The great wing finger was bent backward, and only touched the ground where it fitted upon the wing metacarpal bone. It appears sometimes to have been as long as the entire vertebral column.

Owing to the circumstance that the joint in the arm in Pterodactyles was not at the wrist as among birds, but between the metacarpus and the phalanges, it follows that the fore limb was longer than the hind limb when the metacarpus was long; but the difference would not interfere with the movements of the animal, either upon four feet or on two feet, for in bats and birds the disproportion in length is greater.

HUMERUS OR UPPER ARM BONE

The first bone in the fore-arm, the humerus, is remarkable chiefly for the compressed crescent form of its upper articular end, which is never rounded like the head of the upper arm bone in man, and secondly for the great development of the external process of bone near that end, termed the radial crest. Sir Richard Owen compared the bone to the humerus of both birds and crocodiles, but in its upper articular end the crocodile bone may be said to be more like a bird than it is like the Pterodactyle. In flying reptiles the articular surface next to the shoulder-girdle is somewhat saddle-shaped, being concave from side to side above and convex vertically, while most animals with which it can be compared have the articular head of the bone convex in both directions. A remarkable exception to this general rule is found in some fossil animals from South Africa, which, from resemblance to mammals in their teeth, have been termed Theriodonts. They sometimes have the head of the bone concave from side to side and convex in the vertical direction. To this condition Ornithorhynchus makes a slight approximation. The singular expansion of the structure called the radial crest finds no close parallel in reptiles, though Crocodiles have a moderate crest on the humerus in the same position; and in Theriodonts the radial crest extends much further down the shaft of the humerus. No bird has a radial crest of a similar kind, though it is prolonged some way down the shaft in Archaeopteryx. In Pterodactyles it sometimes terminates outward in a smooth, rounded surface, which might have been articular if any structure could have articulated with it. There is also a moderate expansion of the bone on the ulnar side in some Pterodactyles, so that the proximal end often incloses nearly three-fourths of an ovate outline. The termination of the radial crest is at the opposite end of this oval to the wider articular part of the head of the bone, in some specimens from the Cambridge Greensand. The radial crest is more extended in Rhamphorhynchus. All specimens of the humerus show a twist in the length of the bone, so that the end towards the fore-arm, which is wider than the shaft, makes a right angle with the radial crest on the proximal end, which is not seen in birds. The shaft of the humerus is always stouter than that of the femur, though different genera differ in this respect.

The humerus in genera from rocks associated with the Chalk presents two modifications, chiefly seen in the characters of the distal end of the bone. One of these is a stout bone with a curiously truncated end where it joins the two bones of the fore-arm; and the other is more or less remarkable for the rounded form of the distal condyles. Both types show distinct articular surfaces. The inner one is somewhat oblique and concave, the outer one rounded; the two being separated by a concave channel, so that the ulna makes an oblique articulation with the bone as in birds, and the radius articulates by a more or less truncated or concave surface.

ULNA AND RADIUS

The bones of the fore-arm are similar to each other in size, and if there be any difference between them the ulna is slightly the larger. There is some evidence that in Rhamphorhynchus the upper end of the ulna was placed behind the radius, probably in consequence of the mode of attachment of those bones to the humerus. The ulna abutted towards the inner and lower border, while the radius was towards the upper border, consequent upon the twist in the humerus. This condition corresponds substantially with the arrangement in birds, but differs from birds in the relatively more important part taken by the radius in making the articulation. The bones are compared in Dimorphodon with the Golden Eagle drawn of the same size (Fig. 42). In birds the ulna supports the great feathers of the wing, and this may account for the size of the bone. The ulna is best seen at its proximal end in the specimens from the Cambridge Greensand, where there is a terminal olecranon ossification forming an oblique articulation, which frequently comes away and is lost. It is sometimes well preserved, and indicated by a suture. The examples of ulna from the Lias show a slight expansion of the bone at both ends, and at the distal end toward the wrist the articulation is well defined, where the bone joins the carpus. The larger specimens of the bone are broken. The distal articular surface is only connected with the proximal end of the bone in small specimens: it always shows on the one margin a concavity, followed by a prominent boss, and an oblique articulation beyond the boss. On the side towards the radius, on the lower end of the shaft there is an angular ridge, which marks the line along which the ulna overlaps the radius. The lower end of the radius has a simple, slightly convex articulation, somewhat bean-shaped. No rotation of these bones on each other was possible as in man. There is a third bone in the fore-arm. This bone, named the pteroid, is commonly seen in skeletons from Solenhofen. It was regarded by Von Meyer as having supported the wing membrane in flight. Some writers have interpreted it as an essential part of the Pterodactyle skeleton, and Von Meyer thought that it might possibly indicate a fifth digit in the hand. The only existing structure at all like it is seen in the South African insectivorous mammal named Chrysochloris capensis, the golden mole, which also has three bones in the fore-arm, the third bone extending half-way up towards the humerus. In that animal the third bone appears to be behind the others and adjacent to the ulna. In the German fossils the pteroid articulated with a separate carpal or metacarpal bone, placed on the side of the arm adjacent to the radius, and the radius is always more inward than the ulna. If the view suggested by Von Meyer is adopted, this bone would be a first digit extending outward and backward towards the humerus. That view was adopted by Professor Marsh. It involves the interpretation of what has been termed the lateral carpal as the first metacarpal bone, which would be as short as that of a bird, but turned in the opposite direction backward. The first digit would then only carry one phalange, and would not terminate in a claw, but lie in the line of the tendon which supports the anterior wing membrane of a bird.

The third bone in the fore-arm of Chrysochloris does not appear to correspond to a digit. The bone is on the opposite side of the arm to the similar bone of a Pterodactyle, and therefore cannot be the same structure in the Golden Mole. The interpretation which makes the pteroid bone the first digit has the merit of accounting for the fifth digit of the hand. All the structures of the hand are consistent with this view. The circumstance that the bone is rarely found in contact with the radius, but diverging from it, shows that it plays the same part in stretching the membrane in advance of the arm, that the fifth digit holds in supporting the larger wing membrane behind the arm.

According to Professor Williston, the American toothless Pterodactyle Ornithostoma has but a single phalange on the corresponding first toe of the hind foot, and that bone he describes as long, cylindrical, gently curved, and bluntly pointed. There is some support for this interpretation; but I have not seen any English or German Pterodactyles with only one phalange in the first toe.

The wing in Pterodactyles would thus be stretched between two fingers which are bent backward, the three intermediate digits terminating in claws.

THE CARPUS

The wrist bones in the reptilia usually consist of two rows. In Crocodiles, in the upper row there is a large inner and a small outer bone, behind which is a lunate bone, the remainder of the carpus being cartilaginous. Only one carpal is converted into bone in the lower row. It is placed immediately under the smaller upper carpal. In Chelonians, the turtle and tortoise group, the characters of the carpus vary with the family. In the upper row there are usually two short carpals, which may be blended, under the ulna; while the two under the radius are commonly united. The lower row is made up of several small bones. Lizards, too, usually have three bones in the proximal row and five smaller bones in the distal row.

The correspondence of the distal carpals with the several metacarpal bones of the middle hand is a well-known feature of the structure of the wrist.

Von Meyer remarks that the carpus is made up of two rows of small bones in the Solenhofen Pterodactyles; while in birds there is one row consisting of two bones. The structure of the carpus is not distinct in all German specimens; but in the short-tailed Solenhofen genera the bones in the two rows retain their individuality.

In all the Cretaceous genera the carpal bones of each row are blended into a single bone, so that two bones are superimposed, which may be termed the proximal and distal carpals. One specimen shows by an indication of sutures the original division of the distal carpal into three bones; and the separated constituent bones are very rarely met with. Two bones of the three confluent elements contribute to the support of the wing metacarpal, and the third gives an articular attachment to the bone which extends laterally at the inner side of the carpus, which I now think may be the first metacarpal bone turned backward towards the humerus. The three component bones meet in the circular pneumatic foramen in the middle of the under side of the distal carpal. There is no indication of division of the proximal carpal in these genera into constituent bones.

This condition is somewhat different from birds. In 1873 Dr. Rosenberg, of Dorpat, showed that there is in the bird a proximal carpal formed of two elements, and a distal carpal also formed of two elements. Therefore the two constituents of the distal carpal in the bird which blends in the mature animal with the metacarpus, forming the rounded pulley joint, may correspond with two of the three bones in the Cretaceous Pterodactyle Ornithocheirus.

The width of a proximal carpal rarely exceeds two inches, and that of a distal carpal is about an inch and three-quarters. Two such bones when in contact would not measure more than one inch in depth. The lower surface shows that the wing had some rotary movement upon the carpus outward and backward.

METACARPUS

The metacarpus consists of bones which correspond to the back of the hand. The first digit of the hand in clawed animals has the metacarpal bone short, or shorter than the others. Among mammals metacarpal bones are sometimes greatly elongated; and a similar condition is found in Pterodactyles, in which the metacarpal bone may be much longer than the phalange which is attached to it. Two metacarpal bones appear to be singularly stouter than the others. The first bone of the first digit, if rightly determined, is much shorter than the others, and is, in fact, no longer than the carpus (Fig. 43). It is a flat oblong bone, attached to the inner side of the lower carpal, and instead of being prolonged distally in the same direction as the other metacarpal bones, is turned round and directed upward, so that its upper edge is flush with the base of the radius, and gives attachment to a bone which resembles a terminal phalange of the wing finger. According to this interpretation it is the first and only phalange in the first digit. The bone is often about half as long as the fore-arm, terminates upward in a point, is sometimes curved, and frequently diverges outward from the bones of the fore-arm, as preserved in the associated skeleton, being stretched towards the radial crest of the humerus. This mode of attachment of the supposed first metacarpal, which is true for all Cretaceous pterodactyles, has not been shown to be the same for all those from the Solenhofen Slate. There is no greater anomaly in this metacarpal and phalange on the inner side being bent backward, than there is in the wing finger being bent backward on the outer side. The three slender intervening digits extend forward between them, as though they were applied to the ground for walking.

The bone which is usually known as the wing metacarpal is frequently stouter at the proximal end towards the carpus than towards the phalange. At the carpal end it is oblong and truncated, with a short middle process, which may have extended into the pit in the base of the carpal bone; while the distal terminal end is rounded exactly like a pulley. There is great difference in the length of the metacarpus. In the American genus Ornithostoma it is much longer than the fore-arm. In Rhamphorhynchus it is remarkably short, though perhaps scarcely so short as in Dimorphodon or in Scaphognathus. The largest Cretaceous examples are about two inches wide where they join the carpus. The bone is sometimes a little curved.

Between the first and fifth or wing metacarpal are the three slender metacarpal bones which give attachment to the clawed digits. They bear much the same relation to the wing metacarpal that the large metatarsal of a Kangaroo has to the slender bones of the instep which are parallel to it.

The facet for the wing metacarpal on the carpus is clearly recognised, but as a rule there is no surface with which the small metacarpals can be separately articulated. One or two exceptional specimens from the Cambridge Greensand appear to have not only surfaces for the wing metacarpal, but two much smaller articular surfaces, giving attachment to smaller metacarpals; while in one case there appears to be only one of these additional impressions. It is certain that all the animals from the Lias and Oolites have three clawed digits, but at present I have seen no evidence that there were three in the Cretaceous genera, though Professor Williston's statements and restoration appear to show that the toothless Pterodactyles have three. Another difference from the Oolitic types, according to Professor Williston, is in the length of the slender metacarpals of the clawed phalanges being about one-third that of the wing metacarpal, but this is probably due to imperfect ossification at the proximal end; for at the distal end the bones all terminated on the same level, showing that the four outer digits were applied to the ground to support the weight of the body. The corresponding bone in the Horse and Oxen is carried erect, so as to be in a vertical line with the bones of the fore-arm; and the same position prevails usually, though not invariably, with the corresponding bone in the hind limb, while in many clawed mammals the metacarpus and metatarsus are both applied upon the ground. In Pterodactyles the metatarsal bones are preserved in the rock in the same straight line with the smaller bones of the foot, or make an angle with the shin bone, leading to the conviction that the bones of the foot were applied to the ground as in Man, and sometimes as in the Dog, and were thus modified for leaping. Just as the human metacarpus is extended in the same line with the bones of the fore-arm, and the movement of jointing occurs where the fingers join the metacarpus, so Pterodactyles also had these bones differently modified in the fore and hind limbs for the functions of life. The result is to lengthen the fore limb as compared with the hind limb by introducing into it an elevation above the ground which corresponds to the length of the metacarpus, always supposing that the animal commonly assumed the position of a quadruped when upon the earth's surface.

This position of the metacarpus is a remarkable difference from Birds, because when the bird's wing is at rest it is folded into three portions. The upper arm bone extends backward, the bones of the fore-arm are bent upon it so as to extend forward, and then at the wrist the third portion, which includes the metacarpus and finger bones, is bent backward. So that the metacarpus in the Pterodactyle differs from birds in being in the same line as the bones of the fore-arm, whereas in birds it is in the same line with the digit bones of the hand. It is worthy of remark that in Bats, which are so suggestive of Pterodactyles in some features of the hand, the metacarpals and phalanges are in the same straight line; so that in this respect the bat is more like the bird. But Pterodactyles in the relation of these bones to flight are quite unlike any other animal, and have nothing in common with the existing animals named Reptiles.

THE HAND

From what has just been said it follows that the construction of the hand is unique. It may be contrasted with the foot of a bird. The bone which is called, in the language of anatomists, the tarso-metatarsus, and is usually free from feathers and covered with skin, is commonly carried erect in birds, so that the whole body is supported upon it; and from it the toes diverge outward. It is formed in birds of three separate bones blended together. In the fore limb of the Pterodactyle the metacarpus has the same relation to the bones of the fore-arm that the metatarsus has to the corresponding bones of the leg in a bird. But the three metacarpal bones in the Pterodactyle remain distinct from each other, perhaps because the main work of that region of the skeleton has devolved upon the digit called the wing finger, which is not recognised in the bird. In the Pterodactyles from the Solenhofen Slate there is a progressive number of phalanges in the three small digits of the hand, which were applied to the ground. This number in the great majority of species follows the formula of two bones in the first, three bones in second, and four in the third; so that in the innermost of the clawed digits only one bone intervenes between the metacarpal and the claw. The fingers slightly increase in length with increase in number of bones which form them.

The terminal claw bones are unlike the claws of Birds or Reptiles. They are compressed from side to side, and extremely deep and strong, with evidence of powerful attachment for ligaments, so that they rather resemble in their form and large size the claws of some of the carnivorous fossil reptiles, often grouped as Dinosauria, such as have been termed Aristosuchus and Megalosaurus. In the hand of the Ostrich the first and second digits terminate in claws, while the third is without a claw. But these claws of the Ostrich and other birds are slender, curved, and rather feeble organs. In the Archaeopteryx, a fossil bird which agrees with the Pterodactyles in retaining the separate condition of the metacarpal bones and in having the same number of phalanges in two of the fingers of the fore limb, the terminal claws are rather more compressed from side to side, and stronger than in the Ostrich, but not nearly so strong as in the Pterodactyle. The Archaeopteryx differs from the Pterodactyle in having no trace of a wing finger. The first metacarpal bone is short, as in all birds; and the first phalange scarcely lengthens that segment of the first digit of the Bird's hand to the same length as the other metacarpal bones. It therefore was not bent backward like the first digit in Pterodactyles. The wing finger, from which the genius of Cuvier selected the scientific name--Pterodactyle--for these fossils, yields their most distinctive character. It is a feature which could only be partly paralleled in the Bat, by making changes of structure which would remove every support to the wing but the outermost digit of that animal's hand. In the Bat's hand the membrane for flight is extended chiefly by four diverging metacarpal bones. There are only two or three phalanges in each digit in its four wing fingers. In Pterodactyles the metacarpal bones are, as we have seen, arranged in close contact, and take no part in stretching the wing.

THE WING FINGER

In Birds there is nothing whatever to represent the wing finger of the Pterodactyle, for it is an organ external to the finger bones of the bird, and contains four phalanges. The first phalange is quite different from the others. Its length is astonishing when compared with the small phalanges of the clawed fingers. The articular surface, which joins on to the wing metacarpal bone, is a concave articulation, which fits the pulley in which that bone ends. The pulley articulation admits of an extension movement in one direction only. Many specimens show the wing finger to be folded up so as to extend backward. The whole finger is preserved in other specimens straightened out so as to be in line with the metacarpus. This condition is well seen in Professor Marsh's specimen of Rhamphorhynchus, which has the wing membrane preserved, in which all bones of the fore-arm metacarpus and wing finger are extended in a continuous curve. The outer surface of the end of the first bone of the wing finger overlaps the wing metacarpal, so that a maximum of strength and resistance is provided in the bony structures by which the wing is supported. There is, therefore, in flight only one angular bend in the limb, and that is between the upper arm bone and the fore-arm.

An immense pneumatic foramen is situate in a groove on the under side of the upper end of the first phalange in Ornithocheirus, but is absent in specimens from the Kimeridge clay. This bone is long and stout. It terminates at the lower end in an obliquely truncated articular surface. Specimens occur in the Cambridge Greensand which are 2 inches broad at the upper end and nearly 1-1/2 inch wide at the lower end. An imperfect bone from the Chalk is 14-1/2 inches long. The bones are all flattened. Specimens from the Chalk of Kansas at Munich are 28 inches long. The second phalange is concave at the upper articular end and convex in the longer direction at the lower end. The articular points of union between the several phalanges form prominences on the under side of the finger in consequence of the adjacent bones being a little widened at their junction. It should be mentioned that there is a proximal epiphysis or separate bone to the first phalange, adjacent to the pulley joint of the metacarpal bone, which is like the separate olecranon process of the ulna of the fore-arm. It sometimes comes away in specimens from the Chalk and Cambridge Greensand, leaving a large circular pit with a depressed narrow border. On the outer side of this process is a rounded boss, which may possibly have supported the bone, if it were applied to the ground with the wing folded up, like the wing of a Bat directed upward and backward at the animal's side.

The four bones of the wing finger usually decrease progressively in length, so that in Rhamphorhynchus, in which the length of the animal's head only slightly exceeds 3-1/2 inches, the first phalange is nearly as long, the second phalange is about 3-1/4 inches, the third 2-3/4 inches, and the fourth a little over 2 inches. Thus the entire length of the four phalanges slightly exceeds 11 inches, or rather more than three times the length of the head. But the fore-arm and metacarpus in this type only measure 3 inches. Therefore the entire spread of wings could not have been more than 2 feet 9 inches.

The largest Ornithosaur in which accurate measurements have been made is the toothless Pterodactyle Ornithostoma, also named Pteranodon, from North America. In that type the head appears to have been about 3 or 4 feet long, and the wing finger exceeded 5 feet; while the length of the fore-arm and metacarpus exceeded 3 feet. The width of the body would not have been more than 1 foot. The length of the short humerus, which was about 11 inches, did not add greatly to the stretch of the wing; so that the spread of the wings as stretched in flight may be given as probably not exceeding 17 or 18 feet. A fine example of the wing bones of this animal quite as large has been obtained by the (British Museum Natural History). Many years ago, on very fragmentary materials, I estimated the wings in the English Cretaceous Ornithocheirus as probably having a stretch of 20 feet in the largest specimens, basing the calculation partly upon the extent of the longest wings in existing birds relatively to their bones, and partly upon the size of the largest associated bones which were then known.

CHAPTER XII

EVIDENCES OF THE ANIMAL'S HABITS FROM ITS REMAINS

Such are the more remarkable characters of the bones in a type of animal life which was more anomalous than any other which peopled the earth in the Secondary Epoch of geological time. Its skeleton in different parts resembles Reptiles, Birds, and Mammals; with modifications and combinations so singular that they might have been deemed impossible if Nature's power of varying the skeleton could be limited. Since Ornithosaurs were provided with wings, we may believe the animals to some extent to have resembled birds in habit. Their modes of progression were more varied, for the structures indicate an equal capacity for movement on land as a biped, or as a quadruped, with movement in the air. There is little evidence to support the idea that they were usually aquatic animals. The majority of birds which frequent the water have their bodies stored with fat and the bones of their extremities filled with marrow. And a bird's marrow bones are stouter and stronger than those which are filled with air. There are few, if any, bones of Pterodactyles so thick as to suggest the conclusion that they contained marrow, and the bones of the extremities appear to have been constructed on the lightest type found among terrestrial birds. Their thinness, except in a few specimens from the Wealden rocks, is marvellous; and all the later Pterodactyles show the arrangement, as in birds, by which air from the lungs is conveyed to the principal bones. No Pterodactyle has shown any trace of the web-footed condition seen in birds which swim on the water, unless the diverging bones of the hind foot in Rhamphorhynchus supports that inference. The bones of the hind foot are relatively small, and if it were not that a bird stands easily upon one foot, might be considered scarcely adequate to support the animal in the position which terrestrial birds usually occupy. Yet, as compared with the length and breadth of the foot in an Ostrich, the toes of an Ornithosaur are seen to be ample for support. These facts appear to discourage the idea that the animals were equally at home on land and water, and in air.

Some light may be thrown upon the animal's habits by the geological circumstances under which the remains are found. The Pterodactyle named Dimorphodon, from the Lias of the south of England, is associated with evidences of terrestrial land animals, the best known of which is Scelidosaurus, an armoured Dinosaur adapted by its limbs for progression on land. And the Pterodactyle Campylognathus, from the Lias of Whitby, is associated with trunks of coniferous trees and remains of Insects. So that the occurrence of Pterodactyles in a marine stratum is not inconsistent with their having been transported by streams from off the old land surface of the Lias, on which coniferous trees grew and Dinosaurs lived.

Similar considerations apply to the occurrence of the Rhamphocephalus in the Stonesfield Slate of England. The deposit is not only formed in shallow water, but contains terrestrial Insects, a variety of land plants, and many Reptiles and other animals which lived upon land. The specimens from the Purbeck beds, again, are in strata which yield a multitude of the spoils of a nearly adjacent land surface; while the numerous remains found in the marine Solenhofen Slate in Germany are similarly associated with abundant evidences of varied types of terrestrial life. The evidence grows in force from its cumulative character. The Wealden beds, which yield many terrestrial reptiles and so much evidence of terrestrial vegetation, and shallow-water conditions of disposition, have afforded important Pterodactyle remains from the Isle of Wight and Sussex.

The chief English deposit in which these fossils are found, the Upper Greensand, has afforded thousands of bones, battered and broken on a shore, where they have lain in little associated groups of remains, often becoming overgrown with small marine shells. Side by side with them are found bones of true terrestrial Lizards and Crocodiles of the type of the Gavial of the Indian rivers, many terrestrial Dinosaurs, and other evidences of land life, including fossil resins, such as are met with in the form of amber or copal at the present day.

The great bones of Pterodactyles found in the Chalk of Kent, near Rochester, became entombed, beyond question, far from a land surface. There is nothing to show whether the animals died on land and were drifted out to sea like the timber which is found water-logged and sunken after being drilled by the ship-worm (Teredo) of that epoch. Seeing the power of flight which the animal possessed, storms may have struck down travellers from time to time, when far from land.

Evidence of habit of another kind may be found in their teeth. They are brightly enamelled, sharp, formidable; and are frequently long, overlapping the sides of the jaws. They are organs which are often better adapted for grasping than for tearing, as may be seen in the inclined teeth of Rhamphocephalus of the Stonesfield Slate; and better adapted for killing than tearing, from their piercing forms and cutting edges, in genera like Ornithocheirus of the Greensand. The manner in which the teeth were implanted and carried is better paralleled by the fish-eating crocodile of Indian rivers than by the flesh-eating crocodiles, or Muggers, which live indifferently in rivers and the sea. As the Kingfisher finds its food (see Fig. 20) from the surface of the water without being in the common sense of the term a water bird, so some Pterodactyles may have fed on fish, for which their teeth are well adapted, both in the stream and by the shore.

A Pterodactyle's teeth vary a good deal in appearance. The few large teeth in the front of the jaw in Dimorphodon, associated with the many small vertical teeth placed further backward, suggest that the taking of food may have been a process requiring leisure, since the hinder teeth adapted to mincing the animal's meat are extremely small. The way in which the teeth are shaped and arranged differs with the genera. In Pterodactylus they are short and broad and few, placed for the most part towards the front of the jaws. Their lancet-shaped form indicates a shear-like action adapted to dividing flesh. In the associated genus Rhamphorhynchus the teeth are absent from the extremity of the jaw, are slender, pointed, spaced far apart, and extend far backward. When the jaws of the Rhamphorhynchus are brought together there is always a gap between them in front, which has led to belief that the teeth were replaced by some kind of horny armature which has perished. In the long-nosed English type of Ornithocheirus the jaws are compressed together, so that the teeth of the opposite sides are parallel to each other, with the margins well filled with teeth, which are never in close contact, though occasionally closer and larger in front, in some of the forms with thick truncated snouts.

It is not the least interesting circumstance of the dentition of Pterodactyles that, associated in the same deposits with these most recent genera with teeth powerfully developed, there is a genus named Ornithostoma from the resemblance of its mouth to that of a bird in being entirely devoid of teeth. It is scarcely possible to distinguish the remains of the toothed and toothless skeletons except in the dentary character of the jaws. There is no evidence that the toothless types ever possessed a tooth of any sort. They were first found in fragments in England in the Cambridge Greensand, but were afterwards met with in great abundance in the Chalk of Kansas, where the same animals were named Pteranodon. A jaw so entirely bird-like suggests that the digestive organs of Pterodactyles may in such toothless forms at least have been characterised by a gizzard, which is so distinctive of Birds. The absence of teeth in the Great Ant-eater and some other allied Mammals has transferred the function which teeth usually perform to the stomach, one part of which becomes greatly thickened and muscular, adapting itself to the work which it has to perform. It is probable that the gizzard may be developed in relation to the necessities which food creates, since even Trout, feeding on the shell-fish in some Irish lochs, acquire such a thickened muscular stomach, and a like modification is recorded in other fishes as produced by food.

Closely connected with an animal's habits is the protection to the body which is afforded by the skin. In Pterodactyles the evidence of the condition of the skin is scanty, and mostly negative. Sometimes the dense, smooth texture of the jaw bones indicates a covering like the skin of a Lizard or the hinder part of the jaw of a Bird. Some jaws from the Cambridge Greensand have the bone channeled over its surface by minute blood vessels which have impressed themselves into the bone more easily than into its covering. Thus in the species of Ornithocheirus distinguished as microdon the palate is absolutely smooth, while in the species named machaerorhynchus it is marked by parallel impressed vascular grooves which diverge from the median line. This condition clearly indicates a difference in the covering of the bone, and that in the latter species the covering had fewer blood vessels and more horny protection than in the other. The tissue may not have been of firmer consistence than in the palate of Mammals. The extremity of the beak is often as full of blood vessels as the jaw of a Turtle or Crocodile.

COVERING OF THE BODY

There is no trace even in specimens from the Solenhofen or Stonesfield Slate of any covering to the body. There are no specimens preserved like mummies, and although the substance of the wings is found there is no trace of fur or feathers, bones, or scales on the skin. The only example in which there is even an appearance suggesting feathers is in the beautiful Scaphognathus at Bonn, and upon portions of the wing membrane of that specimen are preserved a very few small short and apparently tubular bodies, which have a suggestive resemblance to the quills of small undeveloped feathers. Such evidences have been diligently sought for. Professor Marsh, after examining the wing membranes of his specimen of Rhamphorhynchus from Solenhofen, stated that the wings were partially folded and naturally contracted into folds, and that the surface of the tissue is marked by delicate striae, which might easily be taken at first sight for a thin coating of hair. Closer investigation proved the markings to be minute wrinkles on the under surface of the wing membrane. This negative evidence has considerable value, because the Solenhofen Slate has preserved in the two known examples of the bird Archaeopteryx beautiful details of the structure of the larger feathers concerned in flight. It has preserved many structures far more delicate. There is, therefore, reason for believing that if the skin had possessed any covering like one of those found in existing vertebrate animals, it could scarcely have escaped detection in the numerous undisturbed skeletons of Pterodactyles which have been examined.

The absence of a recognisable covering to the skin in a fossil state cannot be accepted as conclusive evidence of the temperature, habits, or affinities of the animal. Although Mammalia are almost entirely clothed with dense hair, which has never been found in a recognisable condition in a fossil state in any specimen of Tertiary age, one entire order, the Cetacea, show in the smooth hairless skins of Whales and Porpoises that the class may part with the typical characteristic covering without loss of temperature and without intelligible cause. That the absence of hair is not due to the aquatic conditions of rivers or sea is proved by other marine Mammals, like Seals, having the skin clothed with a dense growth of hair, which is not surpassed in any other order. The fineness of the growth of hair in Man gives a superficial appearance of the skin being imperfectly clothed, and a similar skin in a fossil state might give the impression that it was devoid of hair. There are many Mammals in which the skin is scantily clothed with hair as the animal grows old. Neither the Elephant nor the Armadillo in a fossil state would be likely to have the hair preserved, for the growth is thin on the bony shields of the living Armadilloes. Yet the difficulty need be no more inherent in the nature of hair than in that of feathers, since the hair of the Mammoth and Rhinoceros has been completely preserved upon their skins in the tundras of Siberia, densely clothing the body. This may go to show that the Pterodactyle possessed a thin covering of hair, or, more probably, that hair was absent. Since Reptiles are equally variable in the clothing of the skin with bony or horny plates, and in sometimes having no such protection, it may not appear singular that the skin in Ornithosaurs has hitherto given no evidence of a covering. From analogy a covering might have been expected; feathers of Birds and hair of Mammals are non-conducting coverings suited to arrest the loss of heat.

With the evidence, such as it is, of resemblance of Ornithosaurs to Birds in some features of respiration and flight, a covering to the skin might have been expected. Yet the covering may not be necessary to a high temperature of the blood. Since Dr. John Davy made his observations it has been known that the temperature of the Tunny, above 90 deg. Fahrenheit, is as warm as the African scaly ant-eater named the Pangolin, which has the body more amply protected by its covering. This illustration also shows that hot blood may be produced without a four-celled heart, with which it is usually associated, and that even if the skin in Pterodactyles was absolutely naked an active life and an abundant supply of blood could have given the animal a high temperature.

The circumstance that in several individuals the substance of the wing membrane is preserved would appear to indicate either that it was exceptionally stout when there would have been small chance of resisting decomposition, or that its preservation is due to a covering which once existed of fur or down or other clothing substance, which has proved more durable than the skin itself.

CHAPTER XIII

ANCIENT ORNITHOSAURS FROM THE LIAS

Cuvier's discourse on the revolutions of the Earth made the Pterodactyle known to English readers early in the nineteenth century. Dr. Buckland, the distinguished professor of Geology at Oxford, discovered in 1829 a far larger specimen in the Lias of Lyme Regis, and it became known by a figure published by the Geological Society, and by the description in his famous Bridgewater Treatise, p. 164. This animal was tantalising in imperfect preservation. The bones were scattered in the clay, so as to give no idea of the animal's aspect. Knowledge of its limbs and body has been gradually acquired; and now, for some years, the tail and most parts of the skeleton have been well known in this oldest and most interesting British Pterodactyle.

Sir Richard Owen after some time separated the fossil as a distinct genus, named Dimorphodon; for it was in many ways unlike the Pterodactyles described from Bavaria. The name Dimorphodon indicated the two distinct kinds of teeth in the jaws, a character which is still unparalleled among Pterodactyles of newer age. There are a few large pointed, piercing and tearing teeth in the front of the jaws, with smaller teeth further back, placed among the tearing teeth in the upper jaw; while in the lower jaw the small teeth are continuous, close-set, and form a fine cutting edge like a saw.

The Dimorphodon has a short beak, a deep head, and deep lower jaw, which is overlapped by the cheek bones. The side of the head is occupied by four vacuities, separated by narrow bars of bone. First, in front, is the immense opening for the nostril, triangular in form, with the long upper side following the rounded curve of the face. A large triangular opening intervenes between the nose hole and the eye hole, scarcely smaller than the former, but much larger than the orbit of the eye. The eye hole is shaped like a kite or inverted pear. Further back still is a narrower vertical opening known as the lateral or inferior temporal vacuity. The back of the head is badly preserved. The two principal skulls differ in depth, probably from the strains under which they were pressed flat in the clay. A singular detail of structure is found in the extremity of the lower jaw, which is turned slightly downward, and terminates in a short toothless point. The head of Dimorphodon is about eight inches long.

The neck bones are of suitable stoutness and width to support the head. The bones are yoked together by strong processes. The neck was about 6 inches long, did not include more than seven bones, and appeared short owing only to the depth and size of the head. The length of the backbone which supported the ribs was also about 6 inches. Its joints are remarkably short when compared with those of the neck. The tail is about 20 inches long.

The extreme length of the animal from the tip of the nose to the end of the tail may have been 3 feet 4 inches, supposing it to have walked on all fours in the manner of a Reptile or Mammal. This may have been a common position, but Dimorphodon may probably also have been a biped. Before 1875, when the first restoration appeared in the Illustrated London News, the legs had been regarded as too short to have supported the animal, standing upon its hind limbs. They are here seen to be well adapted for such a purpose. The upper leg bone is 3-1/4 inches long, the lower leg bone is 4-1/2 inches long, and the singularly strong instep bones are firmly packed together side by side as in a leaping or jumping Mammal, and measure 1-1/2 inches in length. Dimorphodon differs from several other Pterodactyles in having the hind limb provided with a fifth outermost short instep bone, to which two toe bones are attached. These bones are elongated in a way that may be compared, on a small scale, with the elongation of the wing finger in the fore limb. The digit was manifestly used in the same way as the wing finger, in partial support of a flying membrane, though its direction may have been upward and outward, rather than inward. There is no evidence of a pulley joint between the metatarsal and the adjacent phalange.

The height of the Dimorphodon, standing on its hind legs in the position of a Bird, with the wings folded upon the body in the manner of a Bird, was about 20 inches. An ungainly, ill-balanced animal in aspect, but not more so than many big-headed birds, and probably capable of resting upon the instep bones as many birds do. The chief point of variation from the Pterodactyle wing is in the relative length of the metacarpus in Dimorphodon. It is shorter than the other bones in the wing, never exceeding 1-1/2 inches. The total length of all the arm bones down to the point where the metacarpus might have touched the ground, or where the wing finger is bent upon it, is about 9 inches, which gives a length of less than 6 inches below the upper arm bone. The four bones of the wing finger measure, from the point where the first bone bends upon the metacarpus, less than 18 inches. So that the wings could only have been carried in the manner of the wings of a Bat, folded at the side and directed obliquely over the back when the animal moved on all fours. Its body would appear to have been raised high above the ground, in a manner almost unparalleled in Reptiles, and comparable to Birds and Mammals. Dimorphodon is to be imagined in full flight, with the body extended like that of a Bird, when the wings would have had a spread from side to side of about 4 feet 4 inches. As in other animals of this group, the three claws on the front feet are larger than the similar four claws on the hind feet; as though the fingers might have functions in grasping prey, which were not shared by the toes.

The restorations give faithful pictures of the skeleton, and the form of the body is built upon the indications of muscular structure seen in the bones.

A second English Pterodactyle is found in the Upper Lias of Whitby. It is only known from an imperfect skull, published in 1888. It has the great advantage of preserving the bones in their natural relations to each other, and with a length of head probably similar to Dimorphodon shows that the depth at the back of the eye was much less; and the skull wants the arched contour of face seen in Dimorphodon. The head has the same four lateral vacuities, but the nostril is relatively small and elongated, extending partly above the oval antorbital opening, which was larger. There is thus a difference of proportion, but it is precisely such as might result from the species having the skull flatter. The head is easily distinguished by the small nostril, which is smaller than the orbit of the eye. The animal is referred to another genus. The quadrate bones which give attachment to the lower jaw send a process inward to meet the bones of the palate, which differ somewhat from the usual condition. Two bony rods extend from the quadrate bones backward and upward to the sphenoid, and two more slender bones extend from the quadrate bones forward, and converge in a #V#-shape, to define the division between the openings of the nostrils on the palate. The #V#-shaped bone in front is called the vomer, while the hinder part is called pterygoid. The bones that extend backward to the sphenoid are not easily identified. This animal is one of the most interesting of Pterodactyles from the very reptilian character exhibited in the back of the head, which appears to be different from other specimens, which are more like a bird in that region. Yet underneath this reptilian aspect, with the bony bar at the side of the temporal region of the head formed by the squamosal and quadrate bones, defining the two temporal vacuities as in Reptiles, a mould is preserved of the cavity once occupied by the brain, showing the chief details of structure of that organ, and proving that in so far as it departs from the brain of a Bird it appears to resemble the brain of a Mammal, and is unlike the brain of a Reptile.

The Pterodactyles from the Lias of Germany are similar to the English types, in so far as they can be compared. In 1878 I had the opportunity of studying those which were preserved in the Castle at Banz, which Professor Andreas Wagner, in 1860, referred to the new genus Dorygnathus. The skull is unknown, but the lower jaw, 6-1/2 inches long, is less than 2-1/2 inches wide at the articulation with the quadrate bone in the skull. The depth of the lower jaw does not exceed 1/4 inch, so that it is in marked contrast to Buckland's Dimorphodon. The symphysis, which completely blends the rami of the jaw, is short. As far as it extends it contains large tearing teeth, followed by smaller teeth behind, like those of Dimorphodon. But this German fossil appears to differ from the English type in having the front of the lower jaw, for about 3/4 inch, compressed from side to side into a sharp blade or spear, more marked than in any other Pterodactyle, and directed upward instead of downward as in Dimorphodon. Nearly all the measurements in the skeleton are practically identical with those of the English Dimorphodon, and extend to the jaw, humerus, ulna and radius, wing metacarpal, first phalange of the wing finger. The principal bones of the hind limb appear to be a little shorter; but the scapula and coracoid are slightly larger. All these bones are so similar in form to Dimorphodon that they could not be separated from the Lyme Regis species, if they were found in the same locality.

Just as the Upper Lias in England has yielded a second Pterodactyle, so the Upper Lias in Germany has yielded a skeleton, to which Felix Plieninger, in 1894, gave the name Campylognathus. It is an instructive skeleton, with the head much smaller than in Dimorphodon, being less than 6 inches long, but, unfortunately, broken and disturbed. A lower jaw gives the length 4-1/2 inches. Like the other Pterodactyles from the Lias, it has the extremity of the beak toothless, with larger teeth in the region of the symphysis in front and smaller teeth behind. The jaw is deeper than in the Banz specimen from the Lower Lias, but not so deep as in Dimorphodon. The teeth of the upper jaw vary in size, and there appears to be an exceptionally large tooth in the position of the Mammalian canine at the junction of the bones named maxillary and intermaxillary.

The nasal opening is small and elongated, as in the English specimen from Whitby. As in that type there is little or no indication of the convex contour of the face seen in Dimorphodon.

The neck does not appear to be preserved. In the back the vertebrae are about 3/10 inch long, so that twelve, which is the usual number, would only occupy a length of a little more than 3-1/2 inches. The tail is elongated like that of Dimorphodon, and bordered in the same way by ossified ligaments. There are thirty-five tail vertebrae. Those which immediately follow the pelvis are short, like the vertebrae of the back. But they soon elongate, and reach a maximum length of nearly 1-1/2 inches at the eighth, and then gradually diminish till the last scarcely exceeds 1/8 inch in length. The length of the tail is about 22 inches; this appears to be an inch or two longer than in Dimorphodon. The longest rib measures 2-1/2 inches, and the shortest 2 inches. These ribs probably were connected with the sternum, which is imperfectly preserved.

The bones of the limbs have about the same length as those of Dimorphodon, so far as they can be compared, except that the ulna and radius are shorter. The wing metacarpal is of about the same length, but the first phalange of the wing finger measures 6-1/4 inches, the second is about 8-1/4 inches, the third 6-1/2 inches, and the fourth 4-3/4 inches; so that the total length of the wing finger was about half an inch short of 2 feet. One character especially deserves attention in the apparent successive elongation of the first three phalanges in the wing finger in Dimorphodon. The third phalange is the longest in the only specimen in which the finger bones are all preserved. Usually the first phalange is much longer than the second, so that it is a further point of interest to find that this German type shares with Dimorphodon a character of the wing finger which distinguishes both from some members of the group by its short first phalange.

The pelvis is exceptionally strong in Campylognathus, and although it is crushed the bones manifestly met at the base of the ischium, while the pubic bones were separated from each other in front. The bones of the hind limb are altogether shorter in the German fossil than in Dimorphodon, especially in the tibia; but the structure of the metatarsus is just the same, even to the short fifth metatarsal with its two digits, only those bones are extremely short, instead of being elongated as in Dimorphodon. It is therefore convenient, from the different proportions of the body, that Campylognathus may be separated from Dimorphodon; but so much as is preserved of the English specimen from the Upper Lias of Whitby rather favours the belief that our species should also be referred to Campylognathus, which had not been figured when the Whitby skull was referred to Scaphognathus by Mr. Newton. It may be doubtful whether there is sufficient evidence to establish the distinctness of the other German genus Dorygnathus, though it may be retained pending further knowledge.

In these characters are grounds for placing the Lias Pterodactyles in a distinct family, the Dimorphodontidae, as was suggested in 1870. This evidence is found in the five metatarsal bones, of which four are in close contact, the middle two being slightly the longest, so as to present the general aspect of the corresponding bones in a Mammal rather than a Bird. Secondly, the very slender fibula, prolonged down the length of the shin bone, which ends in a rounded pulley like the corresponding bone of a Bird. Thirdly, the great elongation of the third wing phalange. Fourthly, the prolongation of the coracoid bone beyond the articulation for the humerus, as in a Bird. And the toothless, spear-shaped beak, and jaw with large teeth in front and small teeth behind, are also distinctive characters.

CHAPTER XIV

ORNITHOSAURS FROM THE MIDDLE SECONDARY ROCKS

RHAMPHOCEPHALUS

THE Stonesfield Slate in England, which corresponds in age with the lower part of the Great or Bath Oolite, yields many evidences of terrestrial life--land plants, insects, and mammals--preserved in a marine deposit. A number of isolated bones have been found of Pterodactyles, some of them indicating animals of considerable size and strength. The nature of the limestone was unfavourable to the preservation of soft wing membranes, or even to the bones remaining in natural association. Very little is known of the head of Rhamphocephalus. One imperfect specimen shows a long temporal region which is wide, and a very narrow interspace between the orbits; with a long face, indicated by the extension of narrow nasal bones. The lower jaw has an edentulous beak or spear in front, which is compressed from side to side in the manner of the Liassic forms, but turned upward slightly, as in Dorygnathus or Campylognathus. Behind this extremity are sharp, tall teeth, few in number, which somewhat diminish in size as they extend backward, and do not suddenly change to smaller series, as in the Lias genera. A few small vertebrae have been found, indicating the neck and back. The sacrum consists of five vertebrae. One small example has a length of only an inch. It is a little narrower behind than in front, and would be consistent with the animal having had a long tail, which I believe to have been present, although I have not seen any caudal vertebrae. The early ribs are like the early ribs of a Crocodile or Bird in the well-marked double articulation. The later ribs appear to have but one head. #V#-shaped abdominal ribs are preserved. Much of the animal is unknown. The coracoid seems to have been directed forward, and, as in a bird, it is 2-1/2 inches long. The humerus is 3-1/2 inches long, and the fore-arm measured 6 inches, so that it was relatively longer than in Dimorphodon. The metacarpus is 1-3/4 inches long. The wing finger was exceptionally long and strong. Professor Huxley gave its length at 29 inches. My own studies lead to the conclusion that the first finger bone of the wing was the shorter, and that although they did not differ greatly in length, the second was probably the longest, as in Campylognathus.

Professor Huxley makes the second and third phalanges 7-3/4 inches long, and the first only about 3/8 inch shorter, while the fourth phalange is 6-1/2 inches. These measurements are based upon some specimens in the Oxford University Museum. There is only one first phalange which has a length of 7-3/4 inches. The others are between 5 and 6 inches, or but little exceed 4 inches; so that as all the fourth phalanges which are known have a length of 6-1/2 inches, it is possible that the normal length of the first phalange in the larger species was 5-1/2 inches. The largest of the phalanges which may be classed as second or third is 8-1/2 inches, and that, I suppose, may have been associated with the 7-3/4 inches first phalange. But the other bones which could have had this position all measure 5-1/2 and 7-3/4 inches. The three species indicated by finger bones may have had the measurements:--

Phalanges of the wing finger _____/_____ | | I. II. III. IV. 7-3/4 8-1/2 [7?] 6-1/2 } length of each bone 5-1/2 7-3/4 5-1/2 [4-1/2?] } in inches. 4-1/2 ---- ---- ---- }

The femur is represented by many examples--one 3-3/4 inches long, and others less than 3 inches long (2-9/10). In Campylognathus, which has so much in common with the jaw and the wing bones in size, the upper leg bone is 2-8/10 inches. Therefore if we assign the larger femur to the larger wing, the femur will be relatively longer in all species of Rhamphocephalus than in Campylognathus. Only one example of a tibia is preserved. It is 3-1/2 inches long, or only 1/10 inch shorter than the bone in Campylognathus, which has the femur 2-8/10 inches, so that I refer the tibia of Rhamphocephalus to the species which has the intermediate length of wing. These coincidences with Campylognathus establish a close affinity, and may raise the question whether the Upper Lias species may not be included in the Stonesfield Slate genus Rhamphocephalus.

The late Professor Phillips, in his Geology of Oxford, attempted a restoration of the Stonesfield Ornithosaur, and produced a picturesque effect (p. 164); but no restoration is possible without such attention to the proportions of the bones as we have indicated.

OXFORD CLAY

A few bones of flying reptiles have been found in the Lower Oxford Clay near Peterborough, and others in the Upper Oxford Clay at St. Ives, in Huntingdonshire. A single tail vertebra from the Middle Oxford Clay, near Oxford, long since came under my own notice, and shows that these animals belong to a long-tailed type like Campylognathus. The cervical vertebrae are remarkable for being scarcely longer than the dorsal vertebrae; and the dorsal are at least half as long again as is usual, having rather the proportion of bones in the back of a crocodile.

LITHOGRAPHIC SLATE

Long-tailed Pterodactyles are beautifully preserved in the Lithographic Limestone of the south of Bavaria, at Solenhofen, and the quarries in its neighbourhood, often with the skeleton or a large part of it flattened out in the plane of bedding of the rock. Fine skeletons are preserved in the superb museum at Munich, at Heidelberg, Bonn, Haarlem, and London, and are all referred to the genus Rhamphorhynchus or to Scaphognathus. It is a type with powerfully developed wings and a long, stiff tail, very similar to that of Dimorphodon, so that some naturalists refer both to the same family. There is some resemblance.

The type which is most like Dimorphodon is the celebrated fossil at Bonn, sometimes called Pterodactylus crassirostris, which in a restored form, with a short tail, has been reproduced in many text-books. No tail is preserved in the slab, and I ventured to give the animal a tail for the first time in a restoration (p. 163) published by the Illustrated London News in 1875, which accompanied a report of a Royal Institution lecture. Afterwards, in 1882, Professor Zittel, of Munich, published the same conclusion. The reason for restoring the tail was that the animal had the head constructed in the same way as Pterodactyles with a long tail, and showed differences from types in which the tail is short; and there is no known short-tailed Pterodactyle, with wrist and hand bones, such as characterise this animal. The side of the face has a general resemblance to the Pterodactyles from the Lias, for although the framework is firmer, the four apertures in the head are similarly placed. The nostril is rather small and elongated, and ascends over the larger antorbital vacuity. The orbit for the eye is the largest opening in the head, so that these three apertures successively increase in size, and are followed by the vertically elongated post-orbital vacuity. The teeth are widely spaced apart, and those in the skull extend some distance backward to the end of the maxillary bone. There are few teeth in the lower jaw, and they correspond to the large anterior teeth of Dimorphodon, there being no teeth behind the nasal opening. The lower jaw is straight, and the extremities of the jaws met when the mouth was closed. The breast bone does not show the keel which is so remarkable in Rhamphorhynchus, which may be attributed to its under side being exposed, so as to exhibit the pneumatic foramina.

The ribs have double heads, more like those of a Crocodile in the region of the back than is the case with the bird-like ribs from Stonesfield. The second joint in the wing finger may be longer than the first--a character which would tend to the association of this Pterodactyle with species from the Lias; a relation to which attention was first drawn by Mr. E. T. Newton, who described the Whitby skull.

The Pterodactyles from the Solenhofen Slate which possess long tails have a series of characters which show affinity with the other long-tailed types. The jaws are much more slender. The orbit of the eye in Rhamphorhynchus is enormously large, and placed vertically above the articulation for the lower jaw. Immediately in front of the eye are two small and elongated openings, the hinder of which, known as the antorbital vacuity, is often slightly smaller than the nostril, which is placed in the middle length of the head, or a little further back, giving a long dagger-shaped jaw, which terminates in a toothless spear. The lower jaw has a corresponding sharp extremity. The teeth are directed forward in a way that is quite exceptional. Notwithstanding the massiveness and elongation of the neck vertebrae, which are nearly twice as long as those of the back, the neck is sometimes only about half the length of the skull.

All these long-tailed species from the Lithographic Stone agree in having the sternum broad, with a long strong keel, extending far forward. The coracoid bones extend outward like those of a Crocodile, so as to widen the chest cavity instead of being carried forward as the bones are in Birds. These bones in this animal were attached to the anterior extremity of the sternum, so that the keel extended in advance of the articulation as in other Pterodactyles. The breadth of the sternum shows that, as in Mammals, the fore part of the body must have been fully twice the width of the region of the hip-girdle, where the slenderer hind limbs were attached. The length of the fore limb was enormous, for although the head suggests an immense length relatively to the body, nearly equal to neck and back together, the head is not more than a third of the length of the wing bones. The wing bones are remarkable for the short powerful humerus with an expanded radial crest, which is fully equal in width to half the length of the bone. Another character is the extreme shortness of the metacarpus, usually associated with immense strength of the wing metacarpal bone.

The hind limbs are relatively small and relatively short. The femur is usually shorter than the humerus, and the tibia is much shorter than the ulna. The bones of the instep, instead of being held together firmly as in the Lias genera, diverge from each other, widening out, though it often happens that four of the five metatarsals differ but little in length. The fifth digit is always shorter.

The hip-girdle of bones differs chiefly from other types in the way in which those bones, which have sometimes been likened to the marsupial bones, are conditioned. They may be a pair of triangular bones which meet in the middle line, so that there is an outer angle like the arm of a capital Y. Sometimes these triangular bones are blended into a curved, bow-shaped arch, which in several specimens appears to extend forward from near the place of articulation of the femur. This is seen in fossil skeletons at Heidelberg and Munich. It is possible that this position is an accident of preservation, and that the prepubic bones are really attached to the lower border of the pubic bones.

Immense as the length of the tail appears to be, exceeding the skull and remainder of the vertebral column, it falls far short of the combined length of the phalanges of the wing finger. The power of flight was manifestly greater in Rhamphorhynchus than in other members of the group, and all the modifications of the skeleton tend towards adaptation of the animals for flying. The most remarkable modification of structure at the extremity of the tail was made known by Professor Marsh in a vertical, leaf-like expansion in this genus, which had not previously been observed (p. 161). The vertebrae go on steadily diminishing in length in the usual way, and then the ossified structures which bordered the tail bones and run parallel with the vertebrae in all the Rhamphorhynchus family, suddenly diverge downward and upward at right angles to the vertebrae, forming a vertical crest above and a corresponding keel below; and between these structures, which are identified with the neural spines and chevron bones of ordinary vertebrae, the membrane extends, giving the extremity of the tail a rudder-like feature, which, from knowledge of the construction of the tail of a child's kite, may well be thought to have had influence in directing and steadying the animal's movements. There are many minor features in the shoulder-girdle, which show that the coracoid, for example, was becoming unlike that bone in the Lias, though it still continues to have a bony union with the elongated shoulder-blade of the back.

The great German delineator of these animals, Von Meyer, admitted six different species. Mr. Newton and Mr. Lydekker diminish the number to four. It is not easy to determine these differences, or to say how far the differences observed in the bones characterise species or genera. It is certain that there is one remarkable difference from other and older Pterodactyles, in that the last or fourth bone in the wing finger is usually slightly longer than the third bone, which precedes it. There is a certain variability in the specimens which makes discussion of their characters difficult, and has led to some forms being regarded as varieties, while others, of which less material is available, are classed as species. I am disposed to say that some of the confusion may have resulted from specimens being wrongly named. Thus, there is a Rhamphorhynchus called curtimanus, or the form with the short hand. It is represented by two types. One of these appears to have the humerus short, the ulna and radius long, and the finger bones long; the other has the humerus longer, the ulna much shorter, and the finger bones shorter. They are clearly different species, but the second variety agrees in almost every detail with a species named hirundinaceus, the swallow-like Rhamphorhynchus. This identification shows, not that the latter is a bad species, but that curtimanus is a distinct species which had sometimes been confounded with the other. While most of these specimens show a small but steady decrease in the length of the several wing finger bones, the species called Gemmingi has the first three bones absolutely equal and shorter than in the species curtimanus, longimanus, or hirundinaceus. In the same way, on the evidence of facts, I find myself unable to join in discarding Professor Marsh's species phyllurus, on account of the different proportions of its limb bones. The humerus, metacarpus, and third phalange of the wing finger in Rhamphorhynchus phyllurus are exceptionally short as compared with other species. Everyone agrees that the species called longicaudus is a distinct one, so that it is chiefly in slight differences in the proportions of constituent parts of the skeleton that the types of the Rhamphorhynchus are distinguished from each other. I cannot quite concur with either Professor Zittel (Fig. 58, 3) or Professor Marsh (Fig. 58, 2) in the expansion which they give to the wing membrane in their restorations; for although Professor Zittel represents the tail as free from the hind legs, while Professor Marsh connects them together, they both concur in carrying the wing membrane from the tip of the wing finger down to the extremity of the ankle joint. I should have preferred to carry it no further down the body than the lower part of the back, there being no fossil evidence in favour of this extension so far as specimens have been described. Neither the membranous wings figured by Zittel nor by Marsh would warrant so much body membrane as the Rhamphorhynchus has been credited with. I have based my restoration (p. 161) of the skeleton chiefly on Rhamphorhynchus phyllurus.

THE SHORT-TAILED TYPES

The Pterodactylia are less variable; and the variation among the species is chiefly confined to relative length of the head, length of the neck, and the height of the body above the ground. The tail is always so short as to be inappreciable. Many of the specimens are fragmentary, and the characters of the group are not easily determined without careful comparisons and measurements. The bones of the fore limb and wing finger are less stout than in the Rhamphorhynchus type, while the femur is generally a little longer than the humerus, and the wing finger is short in comparison with its condition in Rhamphorhynchus. These short-tailed Pterodactyles give the impression of being active little animals, having very much the aspect of birds, upon four legs or two. The neck is about as long as the lower jaw, the antorbital vacuity in the head is imperfectly separated from the much larger nasal opening, the orbit of the eye is large and far back, the teeth are entirely in front of the nasal aperture, and the post-orbital vacuity is minute and inconspicuous. The sternum is much wider than long, and no specimens give evidence of a manubrium. The finger bones progressively decrease in length. The prepubic bones have a partially expanded fan-like form, and never show the triradiate shape, and are never anchylosed. About fifteen different kinds of Pterodactyles have been described from the Solenhofen Slate, mostly referred to the genus Pterodactylus, which comprises forms with a large head and long snout. Some have been placed in a genus (Ornithocephalus, or Ptenodracon) in which the head is relatively short. The majority of the species are relatively small. The skull in Ornithocephalus brevirostris is only 1 inch long, and the animal could not have stood more than 1-1/2 inches to its back standing on all fours, and but little over 2-1/2 inches standing as a biped, on the hind limbs.

A restoration of the species called Pterodactylus scolopaciceps, published in 1875 in the Illustrated London News in the position of a quadruped, shows an animal a little larger, with a body 2-1/2 inches high and 6 to 7 inches long, with the wing finger 4-1/2 inches long. Larger animals occur in the same deposit, and in one named Pterodactylus grandis the leg bones are a foot long; and such an animal may have been nearly a foot in height to its back, standing as a quadruped, though most of these animals had the neck flexible and capable of being raised like the neck of a Goose or a Deer (p. 30), and bent down like a Duck's when feeding.

The type of the genus Pterodactylus is the form originally described by Cuvier as Pterodactylus longirostris (p. 28). It is also known as P. antiquus, that name having been given by a German naturalist after Cuvier had invented the genus, and before he had named the species. There are some remarkable features in which Cuvier's animal is distinct from others which have been referred to the same genus. Thus the head is 4-1/2 inches long, while the entire length of the backbone to the extremity of the tail is only 6-1/2 inches, and one vertebra in the neck is at least as long as six in the back, so that the animal has the greater part of its length in the head and neck, although the neck includes so few vertebrae. Nearly all the teeth--which are few in number, short and broad, not exceeding a dozen in either jaw--are limited to the front part of the beak, and do not extend anywhere near the nasal vacuity. This is not the case with all.

In the species named P. Kochi, which I have regarded as the type of a distinct genus, there are large teeth in the front of the jaw corresponding to those of Pterodactylus, and behind these a smaller series of teeth extending back under the nostril, which approaches close to the orbit of the eye, without any indication of a separate antorbital vacuity. On those characters the genus Diopecephalus was defined. It is closely allied to Pterodactylus; both agree in having the ilium prolonged forward more than twice as far as it is carried backward, the anterior process covering about half a dozen vertebrae, as in Pterodactylus longirostris. A great many different types have been referred to Pterodactylus Kochi, and it is probable that they may eventually be distinguished from each other. The species in which the upper borders of the orbits approximate could be separated from those in which the frontal interspace is wider.

It is a remarkable feature in these animals that the middle bones of the foot, termed instep bones or metatarsals, are usually close together, so that the toes diverge from a narrow breadth, as in P. longirostris, P. Kochi, and other forms; but there also appear to be splay-footed groups of Pterodactyles like the species which have been named P. elegans and P. micronyx, in which the metatarsus widens out so that the bones of the toes do not diverge, and that condition characterises the Ptenodracon (Pterodactylus brevirostris), to which genus these species may possibly be referred. Nearly all who have studied these animals regard the singularly short-nosed species P. brevirostris as forming a separate genus. For that genus Soemmerring's descriptive name Ornithocephalus, which he used for Pterodactyles generally, might perhaps have retained. But the name Ptenodracon, suggested by Mr. Lydekker, has been used for these types.

Some of the largest specimens preserved at Stuttgart and Tuebingen have been named Pterodactylus suevicus and P. Fraasii. They do not approach the species P. grandis in size, so far as can be judged from the fragmentary remains figured by Von Meyer; for what appears to be the third phalange of the wing finger is 7-1/2 inches long, while in these species it is less than half that length, indicating an enormous development of wing, relatively to the length of the hind limb, which would probably refer the species to another genus. Pterodactylus suevicus differs from the typical Pterodactyles in having a rounded, flattened under surface to the lower jaw, instead of the common condition of a sharp keel in the region of the symphysis. The beak also seems flattened and swan-like, and the teeth are limited to the front of the jaw. There appear to be some indications of small nostrils, which look upward like the nostrils of Rhamphorhynchus, but this may be a deceptive appearance, and the nostrils are large lateral vacuities, which are in the position of antorbital vacuities, so that there would appear to be only two vacuities in the side of the head in these animals. The distinctive character of the skeleton in this genus is found in the extraordinary length of the metacarpus and in the complete ossification of the smaller metacarpal bones throughout their length. The metacarpal bones are much longer than the bones of the fore-arm, and about twice the length of the humerus. The first wing phalange is much longer than the others, which successively and rapidly diminish in length, so that the third is half the length of the first. There are differences in the pelvis; for the anterior process of the ilium is very short, in comparison with its length in the genus Pterodactylus. And the long stalk of the prepubic bone with its great hammer-headed expansion transversely in front gives those bones a character unlike other genera, so that Cycnorhamphus ranks as a good genus, easily distinguished from Cuvier's type, in which the four bones of the wing are more equal in length, and the last is more than half the length of the first; while the metacarpus in that genus is only a little longer than the humerus, and much shorter than the ulna. The Pterodactylus suevicus has the neck vertebrae flat on the under side, and relatively short as compared with the more slender and narrower vertebrae of P. Fraasii.

CHAPTER XV

ORNITHOSAURS FROM THE UPPER SECONDARY ROCKS

When staying at Swanage, in Dorsetshire, many years ago, I had the rare good fortune to obtain from the Purbeck Beds the jaw of a Pterodactyle, which had much in common in plan with the Cycnorhamphus Fraasii from the Lithographic Slate, which is preserved at Stuttgart. The tooth-bearing part of this lower jaw is 8 inches long as preserved, extending back 3 inches beyond the symphysis portion in which the two sides are blended together. It is different from Professor Fraas's specimen in having the teeth carried much further back, and in the animal being nearly twice as large. This fragment of the jaw is little more than 1 foot long, which is probably less than half its original length. A vertebra nearly 5 inches long, which is more than twice the length of the longest neck bones in the Stuttgart fossil, is the only indication of the vertebral column. Professor Owen described a wing finger bone from these Purbeck Beds, which is nearly 1 foot long. He terms it the second of the finger. It may be the third, and on the hypothesis that the animal had the proportions of the Solenhofen fossil just referred to, the first wing finger bone of the English Purbeck Pterodactyle would have exceeded 2 feet in length, and would give a length for the wing finger of about 5 feet 3 inches. For this animal the name Doratorhynchus was suggested, but at present I am unable to distinguish it satisfactorily from Cycnorhamphus, which it resembles in the forms both of the neck bones and of the jaw. Very small Pterodactyles are also found in the English Purbeck strata, but the remains are few, and scattered, like these larger bones.

ORNITHODESMUS LATIDENS

The Wealden strata being shallow, fresh-water deposits might have been expected to supply better knowledge of Pterodactyles than has hitherto been available. Jaws of Ornithocheirus sagittirostris have been found in the beds at Hastings, and in other parts of Sussex. Some fragments are as large as anything known. The best-preserved remains have come from the Isle of Wight, and were rewards to the enthusiastic search of the Rev. W. Fox, of Brixton. In the principal specimen the teeth were short and wide, the head large and deep with large vacuities, but the small brain case of that skull is bird-like. The neck bones are 2-1/2 inches long. In the upper part of the back the bones are united together by anchylosis, so that they form a structure in the back like a sacrum, which does not give attachment to the scapula, as in some Pterodactyles from the Chalk, but the bones are simply blended, as in the frigate-bird, allied to Pelicans and Cormorants. And then after a few free vertebrae in the lower part of the back, succeeds the long sacrum, formed in the usual way, of many vertebrae. I described a sacrum of this type from the Wealden Beds, under the name Ornithodesmus, referable to another species, which in many respects was so like the sacrum of a Bird that I could not at the time separate it from the bird type. This genus has a sternum with a strong deep keel, and the articulation for the coracoid bones placed at the back of the keel in the usual way, but with a relation to each other seen in no genus hitherto known, for the articular surfaces are wedge-shaped instead of being ovate; and instead of being side by side, they obliquely overlap, practically as in wading birds like the Heron. I have never seen any Pterodactyle teeth so flattened and shaped like the end of a lancet; and from this character the form was known between Mr. Fox and his friends as "latidens." The name Ornithodesmus is as descriptive of the sternum as of the vertebral column. The wing bones, as far as they are preserved, have the relatively great strength in the fore limb which is found in many of the Pterodactyles of the Cretaceous period, and are quite as large as the largest from the Cambridge Greensand. In the Sussex species named P. sagittirostris the lower jaw articulation was inches wide.

A few Pterodactyles' bones have been discovered in the Neocomian sands of England and Germany, and other larger bones occur in the Gault of Folkestone and the north of France; but never in such association as to throw light on the aspect of the skeleton.

ORNITHOCHEIRUS

Within my own memory Pterodactyle remains were equally rare from the Cambridge Greensand. The late Professor Owen in one of his public lectures produced the first few fragments received from Cambridge, and with a knowledge which in its scientific method seemed to border on the power of creation, produced again the missing parts, so that the bones told their story, which the work of waves and mineral changes in the rock had partly obliterated. Subsequently good fortune gave me the opportunity during ten years to help my University in the acquisition and arrangement of the finest collection of remains of these animals in Europe. Out of an area of a few acres, during a year or two, came the thousand bones of Ornithosaurs, mostly associated sets of remains, each a part of a separate skeleton, described in my published catalogues, as well as the best of those at York and in the British Museum and other collections in London.

The deposit which yields them, named Cambridge Greensand, may or may not represent a long period of time in its single foot of thickness; but the abundance of fossils, obtained whenever the workmen were adequately remunerated for preserving them, would suggest that the Pterodactyles might have lived like sea-birds or in colonies like the Penguins, if it were not that the number of examples of each species found is always small, and the many variations of structure suggested rather that the individuals represent the life of many lands. The collections of remains are mostly from villages in the immediate vicinity of Cambridge, such as Chesterton, Huntingdon Road, Coldham Common, Haslingfield, Barton, Shillington, Ditton, Granchester, Harston, Barrington, stretching south to Ashwell in Bedfordshire on the one hand, as well as further north by Horningsea into the fens. Each appears to be the associated bones of a single individual. The remains mostly belong to comparatively large animals. Some were small, though none have been found so diminutive as the smallest from the Solenhofen Slate. The largest specimens with long jaws appear to have had the head measuring not more than eighteen inches in length, which is less than half the size of the great toothless Pterodactyles from Kansas.

The Cambridge specimens manifestly belong to at least three genera. Something may be said of the characters of the large animals which are included in the genus Ornithocheirus. These fossils have many points of structure in common with the great American toothless forms which are of similar geological age. The skull is remarkable for having the back of the head prolonged in a compressed median crest, which rose above the brain case, and extended upward and over the neck vertebrae, so as to indicate a muscular power not otherwise shown in the group. For about three inches behind the brain this wedge of bone rested on the vertebrae, and probably overlapped the first three neural arches in the neck.

Another feature of some interest is the expansion of the bone which comes below the eye. In Birds this malar or cheek bone is a slender rod, but in these Pterodactyles it is a vertical plate, which is blended with the bone named the quadrate bone, which makes the articulation with the lower jaw in all oviparous animals.

The beak varies greatly in length and in form, though it is never quite so pointed as in the American genus, for there is always a little truncation in front, when teeth are seen projecting forward from a position somewhat above the palate; the snout is often massive and sometimes club-shaped. Except for these variations of shape in the compressed snout, which is characterised by a ridge in the middle of the palate, and a corresponding groove in the lower jaw, and the teeth, there is little to distinguish what is known of the skull in its largest English Greensand fossils from the skull remains which abound in the Chalk of Kansas.

This English genus Ornithocheirus, represented by a great number of species, had the neural arch of the neck bones expanded transversely over the body of the vertebra in a way that characterises many birds with powerful necks, and is seen in a few Pterodactyles from Solenhofen.

It is difficult to resist the conclusion that the neck vertebrae were not usually more than twice to three times as long as those of the back, and it would appear that the caudal vertebrae in the English Cretaceous types were comparatively large, and about twice as long as the dorsal vertebrae. Unless there has been a singular succession of accidents in the association of these vertebrae with the other remains, Ornithocheirus had a tail of moderate length, formed of a few vertebrae as long as those of the neck, though more slender, quite unlike the tail in either the long-tailed or short-tailed groups of Solenhofen Pterodactyles, and longer than in the toothless Pterodactyles of America.

The singular articulation for the humerus at the truncated extremity of the coracoid bone is a character of this group, as is the articulation of the scapulae with the neural arches of the dorsal vertebrae, at right angles to them (p. 115), instead of running over the ribs as in Birds and as in other Pterodactyles.

The smaller Pterodactyles have their jaws less compressed from side to side. The upper arm bone, the humerus, instead of being truncated at its lower end as in Ornithocheirus, is divided into two or three rounded articular surfaces. That for the radius, the bone which carries the wrist, is a distinct and oblique rounded facet, while the ulna has a rounded and pulley-like articulation on which the hand may rotate. These differences are probably associated with an absence of the remarkable mode of union of the scapulae with the dorsal vertebrae. But I have hesitated to give different names to these smaller genera because no example of scapula has come under my notice which is not truncated at the free end. I do not think this European type can be the Nyctodactylus of Professor Marsh, in which sutures appear to be persistent between the bodies of the vertebrae and their arches, because no examples have been found at Cambridge with the neural arches separated, although the scapula is frequently separated from the coracoid in large animals.

The most interesting of all the English Pterodactyle remains is the small fragment of jaw figured by Sir Richard Owen in 1859, which is a little more than two inches long and an inch wide, distinguished by a concave palate with smooth rounded margins to the jaws and a rounded ridge to the beak. It is the only satisfactory fragment of the animal which has been figured, and indicates a genus of toothless Pterodactyles, for which the name Ornithostoma was first used in 1871. After some years Professor Marsh found toothless Pterodactyles in Kansas, and indicated several species. There are remains to the number of six hundred specimens of these American animals in the Yale Museum alone; but very little was known of them till Professor Williston, of Lawrence, in Kansas, described the specimens from the Kansas University Museum, when it became evident that the bones of the skeleton are mostly formed on the same plan as those of the Cambridge Greensand genus, Ornithocheirus. They are not quite identical. Professor Williston adopts for them the name Ornithostoma, in preference to Pteranodon which Marsh had suggested. Both animals have the dagger-shaped form of jaw, with corresponding height and breadth of the palate. The same flattened sides to the snout, converging upwards to a rounded ridge, the same compressed rounded margin to the jaw, which represents the border in which teeth are usually implanted, and in both the palate has the same smooth character forming a single wide concave channel. Years previously I had the pleasure of showing to Professor Marsh the remarkable characters of the jaw, shoulder-girdle bones, and scapulae in the Greensand Pterodactyles while the American fossils were still undiscovered. I subsequently made the restoration of the shoulder-girdle (p. 115). Professor Williston states to me that the shoulder-girdle bones in American examples of Ornithostoma have a close resemblance to those of Ornithocheirus figured in 1891, as is evident from remains now shown in the British Museum. It appears that the Kansas bones are almost invariably crushed flat, so that their articular ends are distorted. The neck vertebrae are relatively stout as in Ornithocheirus. The hip-girdle of the American Ornithostoma can be closely paralleled in some English specimens of Ornithocheirus, though each prepubic bone is triangular in the American fossils as in P. rhamphastinus. They are united into a transverse bar as in Rhamphorhynchus, unknown in the English fossils. The femur has the same shape as in Ornithocheirus; and the long tibia terminates in a pulley. There is no fibula. The sternum in both has a manubrium, or thick keel mass, prolonged in front of its articular facets for the coracoid bones, which are well separated from each other. Four ribs articulate with its straight sides. The animal has four toes and the fifth is rudimentary; there are no claws to the first and second.

From the Niobrara Cretaceous of Western Kansas. Made by Professor Williston. The original has a spread of wing of about 19 feet 4 inches. Fragments of larger individuals are preserved at Munich]

In the restoration which Professor Williston has made the wing metacarpal is long, and in the shortest specimen measures 1 foot 7 inches, and in the longest 1 foot 8 inches. This is exactly equal to the length of the first phalange of the wing finger. The second wing finger bone is 3 inches shorter, the third is little more than half the length of the first, while the fourth is only 6-3/4 inches long, showing a rapid shortening of the bones, a condition which may have characterised all the Cretaceous Pterodactyles. The short humerus, about 1 foot long, and the fore-arm, which is scarcely longer, are also characteristic proportions of Ornithostoma or Pteranodon, as known from the American specimens. Professor Williston gives no details of the remarkable tail, beyond saying that the tail is small and short, and that the vertebrae are flat at the ends, without transverse processes. In the restoration the tail is shorter than in the short-tailed species from the Lithographic Slate, and unlike the tail in Ornithocheirus.

This is the succession of Pterodactyles in geological time. Their history is like that of the human race. In the most ancient nations man's life comes upon us already fully organised. The Pterodactyles begin, so far as isolated bones are concerned, in the Rhaetic strata; perhaps in the Muschelkalk or middle division of the Trias. And from the beginning of the Secondary time they live on with but little diversity in important and characteristic structures, and so far as habit goes, the great Pterodactyles of the Upper Chalk of England cannot be said to be more highly organised than the earlier stiff-tailed genera of the Lias or the Oolites. There is nothing like evolution. No modification such as that which derives the one-toed horse or the two-toed ox from ancestors with a larger number of digits. On the other hand, there is little, if any, evidence of degeneration. The later Pterodactyles do not appear to have lost much, although the tail in some of the Solenhofen genera may be degenerate when compared with the long tail of Dimorphodon; but the short-tailed types are found side by side with the long-tailed Rhamphorhynchus. The absence of teeth may be regarded as degeneration, for they have presumably become lost, in the same way that Birds now existing have lost the teeth which characterised the fossil birds--Ichthyornis of the American Greensand, and Archaeopteryx of the Upper Oolites of Bavaria. But just as some of the earlier Pterodactyles have no teeth at the extremity of the jaw, such as Dorygnathus and Rhamphorhynchus, so the loss of teeth may have extended backward till the jaws became toothless. The specimens hitherto known give no evidence of such a change being in progress. But just as the division of Mammals termed Edentata usually wants only the teeth which characterise the front of the jaw, yet others, like the Great Ant-eater of South America named Myrmecophaga, have the jaws as free from teeth as the toothless Pterodactyles or living Birds, and show that in that order the teeth have no value in separating these animals into subordinate groups any more than they have among the Monotremata, where one type has teeth and the other is toothless.

The following table gives a summary of the Geological History and succession in the Secondary Rocks of the principal genera of Flying Reptiles.

```
---------------------+---------------------------------------- | NAMES OF THE
GENERA. GEOLOGICAL FORMATIONS. +----------------------+---------------------- |
British and European. | North American. ----------------------+----------------------
+---------------------- Upper Chalk | |} Ornithostoma | |} (Pteranodon) Lower
Chalk |} Ornithocheirus |} Nyctodactylus Upper Greensand |} | Ornithostoma
| Gault | | | ----------------------+ | | Lower Greensand | | | Wealden |
Ornithodesmus | Purbeck | Doratorhynchus | ----------------------+ | Portland
|{ Pterodactylus | |{ Ptenodracon | Kimeridge Clay and |{ Cycnorhamphus |
Solenhofen Slate |{ Diopecephalus | |{ Rhamphorhynchus | Coralline Oolite
|{ Scaphognathus | | | Oxford Clay | | ----------------------+ | Great Oolite and
| | Stonesfield Slate | Rhamphocephalus | | | Inferior Oolite | | ------------------
```

```
------+ | Upper Lias |{ Campylognathus |  |{ Dorygnathus | Lower Lias |
Dimorphodon | ----------------------+ | Rhaetic | bones | | | Muschelkalk | ?
bones | ---------------------+--------------------+---------------------
```

CHAPTER XVI

CLASSIFICATION OF THE ORNITHOSAURIA

When an attempt is made to determine the place in nature of an extinct
group of animals and the relation to each other of the different types
included within its limits, so as to express those facts in a classification,
attention is directed in the first place to characters which are constant, and
persist through the whole of its constituent genera. We endeavour to find the
structural parts of the skeleton which are not affected by variation in the
dentition, or the proportions of the extremities, or length of the tail, which
may define families or genera, or species.

It has already been shown that while in many ways the Ornithosaurian
animals are like Birds, they have also important resemblances to Reptiles.
They are often named Pterosauria. The wing finger gives a distinctive
character which is found in neither one class of existing animals nor the other,
and is common to all the Pterodactyles at present known. They have been
named Ornithosauria as a distinct minor division of back-boned animals,
which may be regarded as neither Reptiles nor Birds in the sense in which
those terms are used to define a Lizard or Ostrich among animals which still
exist. It is not so much that they mark a transition from Reptile to Bird, as that
they are a group which is parallel to Birds, and more manifestly holds an
intermediate place than Birds do between Reptiles and Mammals. In plan of
structure Bird and Reptile have more in common than was at one time
suspected. The late Professor Huxley went so far as to generalise on those
coincidences in parts of the skeleton, and united Birds and Reptiles into one
group, which he named Sauropsida, to express the coincidences of structure
between the Lizard and the Bird tribes. The idea is of more value than the
term in which it is expressed, because Reptiles are not, as we have seen, a
group of animals which can be defined by any set of characters as
comprehensive as those which express the distinctive features of Birds. From
the anatomist's point of view Birds are a smaller group, and while some
Reptiles have affinity with them, it is rather the extinct than the living groups

which indicate that relation. Other Reptiles have affinities of a more marked kind with Mammals, and there are points in the Ornithosaurian skeleton which are distinctly Mammalian. So that when the Monotreme Mammals are united with South African reptiles known as Theriodontia, which resemble them, in a group termed Theropsida to express their mammalian resemblances, it is evident that there is no one continuous chain of life or gradation in complexity of structure of animals.

We have to determine whether the Ornithosauria incline towards the Sauropsidan or Bird-Reptile alliance, or to the Mammal-Reptile or Theropsidan alliance. There can be no doubt that the predominant tendency is to the former, with a minor affinity towards the latter.

The Ornithosauria are one of a series of groups of animals, living and extinct, which have been combined in an alliance named the Ornithomorpha. That group includes at least five great divisions of animals, which circle about birds, known as Ornithosauria, Crocodilia, Saurischia, Aves, Ornithischia, and Aristosuchia. Their relations to each other are not evident in an enumeration, but may be shown in some degree in a diagram (see p. 190).

THE ORNITHOMORPHA

The Ornithomorpha arranged in this way show that the three middle groups--carnivorous Saurischia, Aristosuchia, herbivorous Ornithischia--which are usually united as Dinosauria, intervene between Birds and Ornithosaurs; and that the Crocodilia and Ornithosauria are parallel groups which are connected with Birds, by the group of Dinosaurs, which resembles Birds most closely.

The Ornithomorpha is only one of a series of large natural groups of animals into which living and extinct terrestrial vertebrata may be arranged. And the succeeding diagram may contribute to make evident the relations of Ornithosauria to the other terrestrial vertebrata (see p. 191).

Herein it is seen that while the Ornithomorpha approach towards Mammalia through the Ornithosauria, and less distinctly through the Crocodilia, they approach more directly to the Sauromorpha, through the Plesiosaurs and Hatteria; while that group also approaches more directly to the Mammals through the Plesiosaurs and Anomodonts.

After a diagram in the Philosophical Transactions of the Royal Society, 1892.]

The Aristosuchia is imperfectly known, and therefore to some extent a provisional group. It is a small group of animals.

After a diagram in the Philosophical Transactions of the Royal Society, 1892.]

Cordylomorpha are Ichthyosaurs and the Labyrinthodont group. Herpetomorpha include Lacertilia, Homoeosauria, Dolichosauria, Chameleonoidea, Ophidia, Pythonomorpha.

The Sauromorpha comprises the groups of extinct and living Reptiles named Chelonia, Rhynchocephala, Sauropterygia, Anomodontia, Nothosauria, and Protorosauria. These details may help to explain the place which has been given to the Ornithosauria in the classification of animals.

Turning to the Pterodactyles themselves, Von Meyer divided them naturally into short-tailed and long-tailed. The short-tailed indicated by the name Pterodactylus he further divided into long-nosed and short-nosed. The short-nosed genus has since been named Ptenodracon (Fig. 59, p. 167). The long-tailed group was divided into two types--the Rhamphorhynchus of the Solenhofen Slate (Fig. 56, p. 161) and the English form now known as Dimorphodon (Fig. 52, p. 150), which had been described from the Lias.

The Cretaceous Pterodactyles form a distinct family. So that, believing the tail to have been short in that group (Fig. 58), there are two long-tailed as well as two short-tailed families, which were defined from their typical genera Pterodactylus, Ornithocheirus, Rhamphorhynchus, and Dimorphodon.

The differences in structure which these animals present are, first: the big-headed forms from the Lias like Dimorphodon, agree with the Rhamphorhynchus type from Solenhofen in having a vacuity in the skull defined by bone, placed between the orbit of the eye and the nostril. With those characters are correlated the comparatively short bones which correspond to the back of the hand termed metacarpals, and the tail is long, and stiffened down its length with ossified tendons. These characters separate Ornithosaurs with long tails from those with short tails.

The short-tailed types represented by Pterodactylus and Ornithocheirus have no distinct antorbital vacuity in the skull defined by bone. The metacarpal bones of the middle hand are exceptionally elongated, and the tail, which was flexible in both, appears to have been short. These differences in the skeleton warrant a primary division of flying reptiles into two principal groups.

The short-tailed group, which was recognised by De Blainville as intermediate between Birds and Reptiles, may take the name Pterodactylia, which he suggested as a convenient, distinctive name. It may probably be inconvenient to enlarge its significance to comprise not only the true Pterodactyles originally defined as Pterosauria, but the newer Ornithostoma and Ornithocheirus which have been grouped as Ornithocheiroidea.

The second order, in which the wing membrane appears to have had a much greater extent, in being carried down the hind limbs, where the outermost digit and metatarsal are modified for its support, has been named Pterodermata, to include the types which are arranged around Rhamphorhynchus and Dimorphodon.

Both these principal groups admit of subdivision by many characters in the skeleton, the most remarkable of which is afforded by the pair of bones carried in front of the pubes, and termed prepubic bones. In the Pterodactyle family the bones in front of the pubes are always separate from each other, always directed forward, and have a peculiar fan-shaped form with concave sides like the bone which holds a similar position in a Crocodile. In the Ornithocheirus family the prepubic bones appear to have been originally triangular, but were afterwards united so as to form a strong continuous bar which extends transversely across the abdomen in advance of the pubic bones. This at least is the distinctive character in the genus Ornithostoma according to Professor Williston, which in many ways closely resembles Ornithocheirus.

The two families in the long-tailed order named Pterodermata are separated from each other by a similar difference in their prepubic bones. In Dimorphodon those bones are separate from each other, and remain distinct through life, meeting in the middle line of the body in a wide plate. On the other hand, in Rhamphorhynchus the prepubic bones, which are at first triangular and always slender, become blended together into a slight transverse bar, which only differs from that attributed to Ornithostoma in its more slender bow-shaped form.

Thus if other characters of the skeleton are ignored and a classification based upon the structure of the pelvis and prepubic bones, there would be some ground for associating the long-tailed Rhamphorhynchus from the Upper Oolites which is losing the teeth in the front of its jaw with the Cretaceous Ornithostoma, which has the teeth completely wanting; while the long-tailed Dimorphodon would come into closer association with the short-tailed Pterodactylus. The drum-stick bone or tibia in Dimorphodon, with its slender fibula, like that of a Bird, also resembles a Bird in the rounded and pulley-shaped terminal end which makes the joint corresponding to the middle of the ankle bones in man. The same condition of a terminal pulley joint is found in the Cretaceous Pterodactyles. But in the true Pterodactyles and in Rhamphorhynchus there usually is no pulley-shaped termination to the lower end of the drum-stick, for the tarsal bones remain separate from each other, and form two rows of ossifications, showing the same differences as separate Dinosaurs into the divisions which have been referred to, from their Bird-like pelvis and tibio-tarsus, as Ornithischia in the one case, and Saurischia in the other from their bones being more like those of living Lizards.

CHAPTER XVII

FAMILY RELATIONS OF PTERODACTYLES TO ANIMALS WHICH LIVED WITH THEM

Enough has been said of the general structure of Pterodactyles and the chief forms which they assumed while the Secondary rocks were accumulating, to convey a clear idea of their relations to the types of vertebrate animals which still survive on the earth. We may be unable to explain the reasons for their existence, and for their departure from the plan of organisation of Reptiles and Birds. But the evidence has not been exhausted which may elucidate their existence. Sometimes, in problems of this kind, which involve comparison of the details of the skeleton in different animals, it is convenient to imagine the possibility of changes and transitions which are not yet supported by the discovery of fossil remains. If, for example, the Pterodactyle be conceived of as divested of the wing finger, which is its most distinctive character, or that finger is supposed to be replaced by an ordinary digit, like the three-clawed digits of the hand which we have regarded as applied to the ground, where, it may be asked, would the animal type be found which approximates most closely to a Pterodactyle which had been thus modified? There are two possible replies to such a question, suggested by the form of the foot. For the old Bird Archaeopteryx has three such clawed digits, but no wing finger. And some Dinosaurs also have the hand with three digits terminating in claws, which are quite comparable to the clawed digits of Pterodactyles.

The truth expressed in the saying that no man by taking thought can add a cubit to his stature is of universal application in the animal world, in relation to the result upon the skeleton of the exercise of a function by the individual. Yet such is the relation in proportions of the different parts of the animal to the work which it performs, so marked is the evidence that growth has extended in direct relation to use of organs and active life, and that structures have become dwarfed from overwork, or have wasted away from disuse--seen throughout all vertebrate animals, that we may fairly attribute to the wing finger some correlated influence upon the proportions of the animal, as a consequence of the dependence of the entire economy upon each of its parts. Therefore if an allied animal did not possess a wing finger, and did not fly, it might not have developed the lightness of bone, or the length of limb which Pterodactyles possess.

The mere expansion of the parachute membrane seen in so-called flying animals, both Mammals and Reptiles, which are devoid of wings, is absolutely without effect in modifying the skeleton. But when in the Bat a wing structure is met with which may be compared to a gigantic extension of the web foot of the so-called Flying Frog, the bones of the fingers and the back of the hand elongate and extend under the stimulus of the function of flight in the same way as the legs elongate in the more active hoofed animals, with the function of running. Therefore it is not improbable that the limbs shared to some extent in growth under stimulus of exercise which developed the wing finger. And if an animal can be found among fossils so far allied as to indicate a possible representative of the race from which these Flying Dragons arose, it might be expected to be at least shorter legged, and possibly more distinctly

Reptilian in the bones of the shoulder-girdle which support the muscles used in flight. It may readily be understood that the kinds of life which were most nearly allied to Pterodactyles are likely to have existed upon the earth with them, and that flight was only one of the modes of progression which became developed in relation to their conditions of existence. The principal assemblage of terrestrial animals available for such comparison is the Dinosauria. They may differ from Pterodactyles as widely as the Insectivora among Mammals differ from Bats, but not in a more marked way. Comparisons will show that there are resemblances between the two extinct groups which appeal to both reason and imagination.

Dinosaurs are conveniently divided by characters of the pelvis first into the order Saurischia, which includes the carnivorous Megalosaurus and the Cetiosaurus, with the pelvis on the Reptile plan; and secondly the order Ornithischia, represented by Iguanodon, with the pelvis on the Bird plan. It may be only a coincidence, but nevertheless an interesting one, that the characters of those two great groups of reptiles, which also extend throughout the Secondary rocks, are to some extent paralleled in parts of the skeleton of the two divisions of Pterodactyles. This may be illustrated by reference to the skull, pelvis, hind limb, and the pneumatic condition of the bones.

The Saurischian Dinosauria have an antorbital vacuity in the side of the skull between the nasal opening and the eye, as in the long-tailed Ornithosaurs named Pterodermata. In some of the older genera of these carnivorous Dinosaurs of the Trias, the lateral vacuities of the head are as large as in Dimorphodon. But in some at least of the Iguanodont, or Ornithischian Dinosaurs, there is no antorbital vacuity, and the side of the face in that respect resembles the short-tailed Pterodactylia. The skull of a carnivorous Dinosaur possesses teeth which, though easily distinguished from those of Pterodactyles, can be best compared with them. The most striking difference is in the fact that in the Dinosaur the nostrils are nearly terminal, while in the Pterodactyle they are removed some distance backward. This result is brought about by growth taking place, in the one case at the front margin of the maxillary bone so as to carry the nostril forward, and in the other case at the back margin of the premaxillary bone. Thus an elongated part of the jaw is extended in front of the nostril. Hence there is a different proportion between the premaxillary and maxillary bones in the two groups of animals, which corresponds to the presence of a beak in a bird, and its absence in living reptiles. It is not known whether the extremity of the Pterodactyle's beak is a single bone, the intermaxillary bone, such as forms the corresponding toothless part of the jaw in the South African reptile Dicynodon, or whether it is made by the pair of bones called premaxillaries which form the extremity of the jaw in most Dinosaurs. Too much importance may perhaps be attached to such differences which are partly hypothetical, because the extinct Ichthyosaurus, which has an exceptionally long snout, has the two premaxillary bones elongated so as to extend backward to the nostrils. A similar elongation of those bones is seen in Porpoises, which also have a long snout; and the bones are carried back from the front of the head to the nostrils, which are sometimes known as blowholes. But the Porpoise has those premaxillary bones not so much in advance of the bones which carry teeth named maxillary, as placed in the interspace between them. The nostrils, however, are not limited to the extremity of the head in all Dinosaurs. If this region of the beak in Dimorphodon be compared with the corresponding part of a Dinosaur from the Permian rocks, or Trias, the relation of the nostril to the bones forming the beak may be better understood.

In the sandstone of Elgin, usually named Trias, a small Dinosaur is found, which has been named Ornithosuchus, from the resemblance of its head to that of a Bird. Seen from above, the head has a remarkable resemblance to the condition in Rhamphorhynchus, in the sharp-pointed beak and positions of the orbits and other openings. In side view the orbits have the triangular form seen in Dimorphodon, and the preorbital vacuities are large, as in that genus, while the lateral nostrils, which are smaller, are further forward in the Dinosaur. The differences from Dimorphodon are in the articulation for the jaw being carried a little backward, instead of being vertical as in the Pterodactyle, and the bone in front of the nose is smaller. Notwithstanding probable differences in the palate, the approximation, which extends to the Crocodile-like vacuity in the lower jaw, is such that by slight modification in the skull the differences would be substantially obliterated by which the skull of such an Ornithosaur is technically distinguished from such a Dinosaur.

The back of the skull is clearly seen in the Whitby Pterodactyle, and its structure is similar to the corresponding part of such Dinosaurs as Anchisaurus or Atlantosaurus, without the resemblance quite amounting to identity, but still far closer than is the resemblance between the same region in the heads of Crocodiles, Lizards, Serpents, Chelonians. Few of these fossil Dinosaur skulls are available for comparison, and those differ among themselves. The coincidences rather suggest a close collateral relation than prove the elaboration of one type from the other. They may have had a common ancestor.

The Trias rocks near Stuttgart have yielded Dinosaurs as unlike Pterodactyles as could be imagined, resembling heavily armoured Crocodiles, in such types as the genus Belodon. Its jaws are compressed from side to side, as in many Pterodactyles, and the nostrils are at least as far backward as in Rhamphorhynchus. Belodon has preorbital vacuities and postorbital vacuities, but the orbit of the eye is never large, as in Pterodactyles. It might not be worth while dwelling on such points in the skull if it were not that the pelvis in Belodon is a basin formed by the blending of the expanded plates of the ischium and the pubis, into a sheet of bone which more nearly resembles the same region in Pterodactyles than does the ischio-pubic region in other Dinosaurian animals like Cetiosaurus.

The backbone in a few Dinosaurs is suggestive of Pterodactyles. In such genera as have been named Coelurus and Calamospondylus, in which the skeleton is only partially known, the neck vertebrae become elongated, so as to compare with the long-necked Pterodactyles. The cervical rib is often very similar to that type, and blended with the vertebra, as in Pterodactyles and Birds. The early dorsal vertebrae of Pterodactyles might almost be mistaken for those of Dinosaurs. The tail vertebrae of a Pterodactyle are usually longer than in long-tailed Dinosauria.

In the limbs and the bony girdles which support them there is more resemblance between Pterodactyles and Dinosaurs than might have been anticipated, considering their manifest differences in habit. Thus all Dinosaurs have the hip bone named ilium prolonged in front of the articulation for the femur as well as behind it, almost exactly as in Pterodactyles and Birds (see p. 95). There is some difference in the pubis and ischium which is more conspicuous in form than in direction of the bones. There is a Pterodactyle imperfectly preserved, named Pterodactylus dubius, in which the ischium is directed backward and the pubis downward, and the bones unite below the acetabular cavity for the head of the femur to work in, but do not appear to be otherwise connected. In Rhamphorhynchus the connexion between these two thickened bars is made by a thin plate of bone. In such a Dinosaur as the American carnivorous Ceratosaurus the two bars of the pubis and ischium remain separate and diverging, and there is no film of bone extending over the interspace between them. The development of such a bony condition would make a close approximation between the Ornithosaurian pelvis and that of those Dinosaurs which closely resemble Pterodactyles in skull and teeth.

Another pelvic character of some interest is the blending of the pubis and ischium of the right and left sides in the middle line of the body. There are some genera of Dinosaurs like the English Aristosuchus from the Weald, and the American genera Coelurus, Ceratosaurus, and others, in which the pubic bones, instead of uniting at their extremities, are pinched together from side to side, and unite down the lower part of their length, terminating in an expanded end like a shoe, which is seen to be a separate ossification, and probably formed by a pair of ossifications joined in the median line. This small bone, which is below the pubes, and in these animals becomes blended with them, we may regard as a pair of prepubic bones like those of Pterodactyles and Crocodiles, except that they have lost the stalk-like portions, which in those animals are developed to compensate for the diminished length of the pubic bones. The prepubic bones may also be developed in Iguanodon, in which a pair of bones of similar form remains throughout life in advance of the pubes, as in Pterodactyles. In those Dinosauria with the Bird-like type of pelvis the pubic bone is exceptionally developed, sending one process backward and another process forward, so that there is a great gap between these diverging limbs to the bone. In the region behind the sternum to which the ribs were attached, and in front of the pelvis, is a pair of bones in Iguanodon shaped like the prepubic bones of Dimorphodon. They have sometimes been interpreted as a hinder part of the sternum, but may more probably be regarded as a pair of prepubic bones articulating each with the anterior process of the pubis (see Fig. 80). The small bones found at the extremities of the pubes in such carnivorous Dinosaurs as Aristosuchus are blended by bony union with the pubes. The bones in Iguanodon are placed behind the sternal region without any attachment for sternal ribs, and the expanded processes converge forwards from the stalk and unite exactly like the prepubic bones of Ornithosaurs. While this character, on the one hand, may link Pterodactyles with the Dinosaurs, on the other hand it may be a link between both those groups and the Crocodiles, in which the front pair of bones of the pelvis has also appeared to be representative of the prepubic bones of Flying Reptiles (see Fig. 32, p. 98).

The resemblances between Pterodactyles and Dinosaurs in the hind limb are not of less interest, though it is rather in the older Pterodactyles such as Dimorphodon, Pterodactylus, and Rhamphorhynchus that the resemblance is closest with the slender carnivorous Dinosaurs. They never have the head of the thigh bone, femur, separated from its shaft by a constricted neck, as in the Pterodactyles from the Chalk. In many ways the thigh bone of Dinosaurs tends towards being Avian; while that of Pterodactyles inclines towards being Mammalian, but with a tendency to be Bird-like in the older types, and to be Mammal-like in the most recent representatives of the group in the Chalk.

The bones of the leg in Ornithosaurs, known as tibia and fibula, are remarkable for the circumstance first that they resemble Birds in the fibula being slender and only developed in its upper part towards the femur, and secondly that in a genus like Dimorphodon this drum-stick bone has the two upper bones of the ankle blended with the tibia, so as to form a rounded pulley joint which is indistinguishable from that of a Bird (see p. 102). There is a large number of Dinosaurs in which this remarkable distinctive character of Birds is also found. Only, Dinosaurs like Iguanodon, for instance, have the slender fibula as long as the tibia, and contributing to unite with the separate ankle bones of the similarly rounded pulley at the lower end. There are no Birds in which the tarsal bones remain separated and distinct throughout life. But in Pterodactylus from Solenhofen, as in a number of Dinosaurs, especially the carnivorous genera, the bones of the tarsus remain distinct throughout life, and never acquired such forms as would have enabled the ankle bone, termed astragalus, to embrace the extremity of the tibia, as it does in Iguanodon. Thus the resemblance of the Ornithosaur drum-stick is almost as close to Dinosaurs as to Birds.

There is great similarity between Dinosaurs and Pterodactyles seen in the region of the instep, known as the metatarsus. These bones are usually four in number, parallel to each other, and similar in form. They are commonly longer than in Dinosaurs; but among some of the carnivorous Dinosaurs their length approximates to that seen in Pterodactyles. In neither group are the bones blended together by bony union, while they are always united in Birds, as in Oxen and similar even-hoofed mammals. Dinosaurs agree with Pterodactyles in maintaining the metatarsal bones separate, but they differ from them and agree with Birds frequently, in having the number of metatarsal bones reduced to three, as in Iguanodon, though Dinosaurs often have as many as five digits developed.

The toe bones, the phalanges of these digits of the hind limb, are usually longer in Pterodactyles than in Dinosaurs, but they resemble carnivorous Dinosaurs in the forms of their sharp terminal bones for the claws, which are similarly compressed from side to side.

So diverse are the functions of the fore limb in Dinosaurs and Pterodactyles, and so remarkably does the length of the metacarpal region of the back of the hand vary in the long-tailed and short-tailed Ornithosaurs, that there is necessarily a less close correspondence in that region of the skeleton between these two groups of animals; for the Pterodactyle fore limb is modified in relation to a function which can only be paralleled among Birds and Bats; and yet neither of those groups of animals approximates closely in this region of the skeleton to the Flying Reptile. Under all the modifications of structure which may be attributed to differences of function, some resemblance to Dinosaurs may be detected, which is best evident in the upper arm bone, humerus; is slight in the fore-arm bones, ulna and radius; and becomes lost towards the extremity of the limb.

If the tendency of the thigh bone to resemble a Mammalian type of femur (p. 100) is a fundamental, deep-seated character of the skeleton, it might be anticipated that a trace of Mammalian character would also be found in the humerus. For what the character is worth, the head of the humerus does show a closer approximation to a Monotreme Mammal than is seen in Birds, and is to some extent paralleled in those South African reptiles which approximate to Mammals most closely. Not the least remarkable of the many astonishing resemblances of these light aerial creatures to the more heavy bodied Dinosaurs is the circumstance that the humerus in both groups makes a not dissimilar approach to that of certain Mammals.

These illustrations may be accepted as demonstrating a relationship between the Ornithosaurs and Dinosaurs now compared, which can only be explained as results of influence of a common parentage upon the forms of the bones. But more interesting than resemblances of that kind is the similarity that may be traced in the way in which air is introduced into cavities in the bones in both groups. In some of the imperfectly known Dinosaurs, like Aristosuchus, Coelurus, and Thecospondylus, the bone texture is as thin as in Pterodactyles, and the vertebrae are excavated by pneumatic cavities, which are amazing in size when compared with the corresponding structures in birds, for the vertebra is often hollowed out so that nothing remains but a thin external film like paper for its thickness. In the Dinosaurian genus Coelurus this condition is as well marked in the tail and back as it is in the neck. The essential difference from Birds appears to be that in the larger carnivorous Dinosaurs the pneumatic condition of the bones is confined to the vertebral column; while Birds and Pterodactyles have the pneumatic condition more conspicuously developed in the limb bones. The pneumatic skeleton, however, appears to be absent from the herbivorous types like Iguanodon and all Dinosaurs which have the Bird-like form of pelvis, and are most Bird-like in the forms of bones of the hind limb. It is possible that some of the carnivorous Dinosaurs also possessed limb bones with pneumatic cavities. Many of those bones are hollow with very thin walls. If their cavities were connected with the lungs the foramina are inconspicuous and unlike the immense holes seen in the sides of the vertebrae.

According to the late Professor Marsh, the limbs of Coelurus and its allies, which at present are imperfectly known, are in some cases pneumatic. Therefore there is a closer fundamental resemblance between some carnivorous Dinosaurs and Pterodactyles than might have been anticipated. But the skull of Coelurus is unknown, and the fragments of the skeleton hitherto published are insufficient to do more than show that the two types were near in kindred, though distinct in habit. Each has elaborated a skeleton which owes much to the common stock which transmitted the vital organs, and the tendency of the bones to take special forms; but which also owes more than can be accurately measured to the action of muscles in shaping the bones and the influence of the mechanical conditions of daily life upon the growth of the bones in both of these orders of animals. Enough is known to prove that all Dinosaurs cannot be regarded as Ornithosaurs which have not acquired the power of flight; though the evidence would lead us to believe that the primitive Ornithosaur was a four-footed animal, before the wing finger became developed in the fore limb as a means of extending a patagial membrane, like the membrane which in the hind limb of

Dimorphodon has bent the outermost digit of the foot upward and outward to support the corresponding organ of flight extending down the hind legs.

It may thus be seen that the characters of Ornithosaurs which have already been spoken of as Reptilian, as distinguished from the resemblances to Birds, may now with more accuracy be regarded as Dinosaurian. The Dinosaurs, like Pterodactyles, must be regarded as intermediate in some respects between Reptiles and Birds. The resemblances enumerated would alone constitute a partial transition from the Reptile to the Bird, although no Dinosaurs have organs of flight; many are heavily armoured with plates of bone, and few, if any, approximate in the technical parts of the skeleton to the Bird class, except in the hind limbs. Yet Dinosaurs have sometimes been regarded as standing to Birds in the relation of ancestors, or as parallel to an ancestral stock.

Before an attempt can be made to estimate the mutual relation of the Flying Reptiles to Dinosaurs on the one hand, and to Birds on the other, it may be well to remember that the resemblance of such a Dinosaur as Iguanodon to a Bird in its pelvis and hind limb is not more remarkable than that of Pterodactyles to Birds in the shoulder-girdle and bones of the fore limb. The keeled sternum, the long, slender coracoid bones and scapulae, are absolutely Bird-like in most Ornithosaurs; and that region of the skeleton only differs from Birds in the absence of a furculum which represents the clavicles, and is commonly named the "merry-thought." The elongated bones of the fore-arm and the hand, terminating in three sharp claws, are characters in which the fossil bird Archaeopteryx resembles the Pterodactyle Rhamphorhynchus, a resemblance which extends to a similar elongation of the tail. It is remarkable that the resemblance should be so close, since Archaeopteryx affords the only bird's skeleton known to be contemporary which can be compared with the Solenhofen Flying Reptiles. The resemblance may possibly be closer than has been imagined. The back of the head of Archaeopteryx is imperfectly preserved in the region of the quadrate bone, malar arch, and temporal vacuity. And till these are better known it cannot be affirmed that the back of the head is more Reptilian in Pterodactyles than in the oldest Birds. The side of the head in Archaeopteryx is distinguished by the nostril being far forward, the vacuity in front of the orbit being as large as in the Pterodactyle Scaphognathus from Solenhofen and other long-tailed Pterodactyles.

CHAPTER XVIII

HOW PTERODACTYLES MAY HAVE ORIGINATED

Ornithosauria have many characters inseparably blended together which are otherwise distinctive of Reptiles, Birds, and Mammals, and associated with peculiar structures which are absent from all other animals. They are not quite alone in this incongruous combination of different types of animals in the same skeleton. Dinosaurs, which were contemporary with Ornithosaurs, approximate to them in blending characters of Birds with the structure of a Reptile and something of a Mammal in one animal. If an Ornithosaur is Reptilian in its backbone, in the articular ends of each vertebra having the cup in front and ball behind in the manner of Crocodiles, Serpents, and many Lizards, a Dinosaur like Iguanodon, which had the reversed condition of ball in front and cup behind in its early vertebrae, may be more Mammalian than Avian in a corresponding resemblance of the bones to the neck in hoofed Mammals. But while Pterodactyles are sometimes Mammalian in having the head of the thigh bone moulded as in carnivorous Mammals and Man, the corresponding bone in a Dinosaur is more like that of a Bird. And while the Pterodactyle shoulder-girdle is often absolutely Bird-like, that region in Dinosaurs can only be paralleled among Reptiles.

Such combinations of diverse characters are not limited to animals which are extinct. There were not wanting scientific men who regarded the Platypus of Australia, when first sent to Europe, as an ingenious example of Eastern skill, in which an animal had been compounded artificially by blending the beak of a Bird with the body of a Mammal. Fuller knowledge of that remarkable animal has continuously intensified wonder at its combination of Mammal, Bird, and Reptile in a single animal. It has broken down the theoretical divisions between the higher Vertebrata, demonstrating that a Mammal may lay eggs like a Reptile or Bird, that the skull may include the reptilian characters of the malar arch and pre-frontal and post-frontal bones, otherwise unknown in Mammals and Birds. The groups of Mammals, Birds, and Reptiles now surviving on the earth prove to be less sharply defined from each other when the living and extinct types are considered together. But in Pterodactyles, Mammal Bird and Reptile lose their identity, as three colours would do when unequally mixed together.

This mingling of characteristics of different animals is not to be attributed to interbreeding, but is the converse of the combination of characters found in hybrid animals. It is no exaggeration to say that there is a sense in which Mammal, Bird, Reptile, and the distinctive structures of the Ornithosaur, have simultaneously developed from one egg, in the body of one animal.

The differences between those vertebrate types of animals consist chiefly in the way in which their organisation is modified, by one strain of characters being eliminated so that another becomes predominant, while a distinctive set of structures is elaborated in each class of animals. The earlier geological history of the higher Vertebrata is very imperfectly known, but the evidence tends to the inference that the older representatives of the several classes approximate to each other more closely than do their surviving representatives, so that in still earlier ages of time the distinction between them had not become recognisable. The relation of the great groups of animals to each other, among Vertebrata, is essentially a parallel relation, like the colours of the solar spectrum, or the parallel digits of the hand. It was natural, when only the surviving life on the earth was known, to imagine that animals were connected in a continuous chain by successive descent, but Mammals have given no evidence of approximation to Birds; and Birds discover no evidence that their ancestors were Reptiles, in the sense in which that word is used to define animals which now exist on the earth. When the variation which animals attain in their maturity and exhibit in development from the egg was first realised, it was imagined that Nature, by slow summing up and accumulation of differences which were observed, would so modify one animal type that it would pass into another. There is little evidence to support belief that the changes between the types of life have been wrought in that way. The history of fossil animals has not shown transitions of this kind from the lower to higher Vertebrata, but only intermediate, parallel groups of animals, analogous to those which survive, and distinct from them in the same way as surviving groups are distinct from each other. The circumstance that Mammals, Birds, and Reptiles are all known low down in the Secondary epoch of geological time, is favourable to the idea of their history being parallel rather than successive. Such a conception is supported by the theory of elimination of characters from groups of animals as the basis of their differentiation. This loss appears always to be accompanied by a corresponding gain of characters, which is more remarkable in the soft, vital organs than in the skeleton. The gain in higher Vertebrates in the bones is chiefly in the perfection of joints at their extremities; but the gain in brain, lungs, heart, and other soft parts is an elaboration of those structures and an increase in amount of tissue.

The resemblances of Ornithosaurs to Mammals are the least conspicuous of their characters. Those seen in the upper arm bone and thigh bone are manifestly not derived from Mammals. They cannot be explained as adaptations of the bones to conditions of existence, because there is no community of habit to be inferred between Pterodactyles and Mammals, in which the bones are in any way comparable.

Other fossil animals show that a fundamentally Reptilian structure is capable of developing in the Mammalian direction in the skull, backbone, shoulder-girdle, hip-girdle, and limbs, so as to be uniformly Mammalian in its tendencies. This is proved by tracing the North American Texas fossils named Labyrinthodonts, through the South African Theriodonts, towards the Monotremata and other Mammalia. Just as those animals have obliterated all traces of the Bird from their skeletons, Birds have obliterated the distinctive characters of Mammals. The Ornithosaur has partially obliterated both. With a skull and backbone marked by typical characters of the Reptile, it combines the shoulder-girdle and hip-girdle of a Bird, with characters in the limbs which suggest both those types in combination with Mammals.

The bones have been compared in the skeleton of each order of existing Reptiles, and found to show side by side with their peculiar characters not only resemblances to the other Reptilia, but an appreciable number of Mammalian and Avian characters in their skeletons. The term "crocodile," for example, indicates an animal in which the skeleton is dominated by one set of peculiar characters. Crocodiles retain enough of the characteristics of several other orders of reptiles to show that an animal sprung from the old Crocodile stock might diverge widely from existing Crocodiles by intensifying what might be termed its dormant characters in the Crocodile skeleton. Comparing animals together bone by bone it is possible to value the modifications of form which they put on, and the resemblances between them, so as to separate the inherited wealth of an animal's affinities with ancestors or collateral groups, from the peculiar characters which have been acquired as an increase based upon its typical bony possessions or osteological capital.

There is no part of the Pterodactyle skeleton which is more distinctly modified than the head of the upper arm bone, which fits into the socket between the coracoid bone and the shoulder-blade. The head of the humerus, as the articular part is named, is somewhat crescent-shaped, convex on its inner border, and a little concave on its outer border, and therefore unlike the ball-shaped head of the upper arm bone in Man and the higher Mammals. It is much more nearly paralleled in the little group of Monotremata allied to the living Ornithorhynchus. In that sense the head of the humerus in a Pterodactyle has some affinity with the lowest Mammalia, which approach nearest to Reptiles. The character might pass unregarded if it were not found in more striking development in fossil Reptiles from Cape Colony, which from having teeth like Mammals are named Theriodontia. In several of those South African reptiles the upper arm bone approaches closer to the humerus in Ornithosaurs than to Ornithorhynchus. Such coincidences of structure are sometimes dismissed from consideration and placed beyond investigation by being termed adaptive modifications; but there can be no hope of finding community of habit between the burrowing Monotreme, the short-limbed Theriodont, and the flying Pterodactyle which might have caused this articular part of the upper arm bone to acquire a form so similar in animals constructed so differently. If the resemblance in the humerus to Monotremes in this respect is not to be attributed to burrowing, neither can the crescent form of its upper articulation be attributed to flight; for in Birds the head of the bone is compressed, but always convex, and Bats fly without any approach to the Pterodactyle form in the head of the humerus. This apparently trivial character may from such comparisons be inferred to be something which the way of life of the animal does not sufficiently account for. These deepest-seated parts of the limbs are slow to adapt themselves to changing circumstances of existence, and retain their characters with moderate variation of the bones in each of the orders or classes of animals. It therefore is safer to regard Mammalian characters, as well as the resemblances which Pterodactyles show to other kinds of animals, as due to inheritance from a time when there was a common stock from which none of these animals which have been considered had been distinctly elaborated.

A few characters of Ornithosaurs are regarded as having been acquired, because they are not found in any other animals, or have been developed only in a portion of the group. The most obvious of these is the elongated wing finger; but in some genera, like Dimorphodon, there is also a less elongation of the fifth digit of the foot, and perhaps in all genera there is a backward development of the first digit of the hand, which is without a claw, and therefore unlike the clawed digit of a Bat. An acquired character of another kind, which is limited to the Cretaceous genera, is seen in the shoulder-blade being directed transversely outward, so that its truncated end articulates by a true joint with the early vertebrae of the back, and defended the cavity inclosed by the ribs by a strong bony external arch. And finally, as the animals later in time acquire short tails, and relatively longer limbs, the bones of the back of the hand, termed metacarpals, acquire greater and distinctive length, which is not seen in the long-tailed types like Rhamphorhynchus.

These and such-like acquired characters distinguish the class of animals from all groups with which it may be compared, and mark the possible limits of variation of the skeleton within the boundary of the order. But no further variation of these parts of the skeleton could make a transition to another order of animals, or explain how the Pterodactyles came into existence, because the characters which separate orders and classes of animals from each other differ in kind from those which separate smaller groups, named genera and species, of which the order is made up. The accumulation of the characters of genera will not sum up into the characters of an order or class.

In making the division of Vertebrate animals into classes the skeleton is often almost ignored. Its value is entirely empirical and based upon the observed association of the various forms of bones with the more important characters of the brain and other vital organs. What is understood as a Mammalian or Avian character in the skeleton is the form of bone which is found in association with the soft vital organs which constitute an animal a Mammal or a Bird.

The characters which theoretically define a Mammal appear to be the enormous overgrowth of the cerebral hemispheres of the brain by which the cerebrum comes into contact with the cerebellum, as among Birds. This character distinguishes both groups of animals from all Reptiles, recent and fossil. But in examining the mould of the interior of the brain case it is rare to have the bones fitting so closely to the brain as to prove that the lateral expansion below the cerebrum and cerebellum is formed by the optic lobes of the brain. Otherwise the brain of a Pterodactyle might be as like to the brain of Ornithorhynchus as it is like that of a Bird (Fig. 19). But it is precisely in this condition of arrangement of the parts of the brain that the specimens appear to be most clear. The lateral mass of brain in specimens of Ornithosaurs from the Lower Secondary rocks appears to be transversely divided into back and front parts, which may be thought to correspond to the structures in a Mammal brain named corpora quadrigemina, but to be placed as the optic lobes are placed in Birds, and to have relatively greater dimensions than in Mammals. No evidence has been observed of this transverse division of the optic lobes of the brain in Pterodactyles from the Chalk and Cretaceous rocks, and so far as the evidence goes this part of the brain was shaped as in birds, but rather smaller.

The brain is the only soft organ in which a Mammalian character could be evidenced. The uniformity in character of the brain throughout the group in Mammals is remarkable, in reference to the circumstance that the reproduction varies in type; the lowest, or Monotreme division, being oviparous. If there is no necessary connexion between the Mammalian brain and the prevalent condition under which the young are produced alive, it may be affirmed also that there is no necessary connexion between the form of the brain and the form of the bones, since the brain cavity in Theriodont reptiles shows no resemblance to that of a Mammal, while the bones are in so many respects only paralleled among Monotremata and Mammalia. The variety of forms which the existing Mammalian orders of animals assume, shows the astonishing range of structure of the skeleton which may coexist with the Mammalian brain. And therefore we are led to the conclusion that any other fundamental modification of brain--such as distinguishes the class of Birds--might also be associated with forms and structures of the skeleton which would vary in similar ways. In other words, if for convenience we define a Mammal by its form of brain, structure of the heart and lungs, and provision for nutrition of the young, without regard to the covering of the skin, which varies between the scales of a pangolin and the practically naked skin of the whale--a bird might be also defined by its peculiar conditions of brain and lungs, without reference to the feathered condition of the skin, though the feathered condition extends backward in time to the Upper Secondary rocks, as seen in the Archaeopteryx.

The Avian characters of Pterodactyles are the predominant parts of their organisation, for the conditions of the brain and lungs shown by the moulds of the brain case and the thin hollow bones with conspicuous pneumatic foramina, give evidence of a community of vital structures with Birds, which is supported by characters of the skeleton. If any classificational value can be associated with the distribution of the pneumatic foramina as tending to establish membership of the same class for animals fashioned on the same plan of soft organs, the evidence is not weakened when a community of structures is found to extend among the bones to such distinctive parts of the skeleton as the sternum, shoulder-girdle, bones of the fore-arm and fore-leg; for in all these regions the Pterodactyle bones are practically indistinguishable from those of Birds. This is the more remarkable because other parts of the skeleton, such as the humerus and pelvis, show a partial resemblance to Birds, while the parts which are least Avian, like the neck bones, have no tendency to vary the number of the vertebrae, in the way which is common among Birds, following more closely the formula of the seven cervical vertebrae of Mammals.

It would therefore appear from the vital community of structures with Birds, that Pterodactyles and Birds are two parallel groups, which may be regarded as ancient divergent forks of the same branch of animal life, which became distinguished from each other by acquiring the different condition of the skin, and the structures which were developed in consequence of the bony skeleton ministering to flight in different ways; and with different habit of terrestrial progression, this extinct group of animals acquired some modifications of the skeleton which Birds have not shown. There is nothing to suggest that Pterodactyles are a branch from Birds, but their relation to Birds is much closer, so far as the skeleton goes, than is their relation with the flightless Dinosaurs, with which Birds and Pterodactyles have many characters in common.

On the theory of elimination of character which I have used to account for the disappearance of some Mammalian characters from the Pterodactyle, that loss is seen chiefly in the removal of the parts which have left a Reptilian articulation of the lower jaw with the skull, and the articulation of the vertebrae throughout the vertebral column by a modified cup-and-ball form of joint. The furculum of the Bird is always absent from the Pterodactyle. No specimen has shown recognisable clavicles or collar-bones. Judged by the standard of existing life, Pterodactyles belong to the same group as Birds, on the evidence of brain and lungs, but they belong to a different group on account of the dissimilar modifications of the skeleton and apparent absence of feathers from the skin.

The most impressive facts in the Pterodactyle skeleton, in view of these affinities, are the structures which it has in common with Reptiles. Some structures are fundamental, like the cup-and-ball articulation of the vertebrae, which is never found in birds or mammals. Although not quite identical with the condition in any Reptile, this structure is approximately Lizard-like or Crocodile-like in the cup-and-ball character. It shows that the deepest-seated part of the skeleton is Reptile-like, though it may not be more Reptilian than is the vertebral column of a Mammal, if comparison is made between Mammals and extinct groups of animals known as Reptiles, such as Dinosaurs and Theriodontia.

The orders of animals which have been included under the name Reptilia comprise such different structural conditions of the parts of the skeleton which may be termed reptilian in Ornithosaurs, that there is good reason for regarding the cup-and-ball articulation as quite a distinctive Reptilian specialisation, in the same sense that the saddle-shaped articulation between the bodies of adjacent vertebrae in a bird is an Avian specialisation. From the theoretical point of view the Ornithosaur acquired its Reptilian characters simultaneously with its Avian and Mammalian characters.

There is nothing in the structure of the skeleton of the Dinosauria, to which Ornithosaurs approximate in several parts of the body, which would help to explain the cup-and-ball articulation of the backbone, if the Flying Reptile were supposed to be an offshoot from the carnivorous Dinosaurs.

The elimination of Reptile characters from so much of the skeleton, and the substitution for them of the characters of Birds and Mammals, would be of exceptional interest if there had been any ground for regarding the flying animal as more nearly related to a Reptile than to a Bird. But if the evidence from the form of the brain and nature of the pneumatic organs seen in the limb bones accounts for the Avian features of the skeleton, the Reptilian condition of the vertebral column helps to show a capacity for variation, and that the fixity of type and structure, which the skeleton of the modern Bird has attained, is not necessarily limited to or associated with the vital organs of Birds.

The variation of the cup-and-ball articulation in the neck of a Chelonian, which makes the third vertebra cupped behind, the fourth bi-convex, the fifth cupped in front, and the sixth flattened behind, shows that too much importance may be attached to the mode of union of these bones in Serpents, Crocodiles, and those Lizards which have the cup in front; for while in Lizards the anterior cup, oblique and depressed, is found in most of its groups, the Geckos show no trace of the cup-and-ball structure, and in that respect resemble the Hatteria of New Zealand.

If, therefore, the cup-and-ball articulation of vertebrae in Ornithosauria has any significance as a mark of affinity to Reptiles, it could only be in approximation to those living Reptiles which possess the same character, and would have it on the hypothesis that both have preserved the structure by descent from an earlier type of animal. This hypothesis is negatived by the fact that the cup-and-ball articulation is unknown in the older fossil Reptiles.

Although the articulation for the lower jaw with the skull in Ornithosaurs is only to be paralleled among Reptiles, the structure is adapted to a brain case which is practically indistinguishable from that of a Bird, except for the postorbital arch.

The hypothesis of descent, therefore, becomes impossible, in any intelligible form, in explanation of distinctive character of the skeleton. The hypothesis of elimination may also seem to be insufficient, unless the potential capacity for new development be recognised as concurrent, and as capable of modifying each region of the skeleton, or hard parts of the animal, in the same way that the soft organs may be modified. From which we infer that all structures, which distinguish the several grades of organisation in modern classifications, soft parts and hard parts alike, may come into existence together, in so far as they are compatible with each other, in any class or ordinal division of animals.

Although the young Mammal passes through a stage of growth in which the brain may be said to be Reptilian, there is no good ground for inferring that Mammal or Bird type of skeleton was developed later in time than that of Reptiles. The various types of Fishes have the brains in general so similar to those of Reptiles that it is more intelligible for all the vertebrate forms of brain to have differentiated at the same time, under the law of elimination of characters, than that there should be any other bond of union between the classes of animals.

If we ask what started the Ornithosauria into existence, and created the plan of construction of that animal type, I think science is justified in boldly affirming that the initial cause can only be sought under the development of patagial membranes, such as have been seen in various animals ministering to flight. Such membranes, in an animal which was potentially a Bird in its vital organs, have owed development to the absence of quill feathers. Thus the wing membrane may be the cause for the chief differences of the skeleton by which Ornithosaurs are separated from Birds, for the stretch of wing in one case is made by the skin attached to the bones, and in the other case by feathers on the skin so attached as to necessitate that the wing bones have different proportions from Ornithosaurs.

It is a well-known observation that each great epoch of geological time has had its dominant forms of animal life, which, so far as the earth's history is known now, came into existence, lived their time, and were seen no more. In the same way the smaller groups of species and genera included in an ordinal group of animals or class have abounded, giving a tone to the life of each geological formation, until the vitality of the animal is exhausted, and the species becomes extinct or ceases to preponderate. This process is seen to be still modifying the life on the earth, when some kinds of animals and plants are introduced to new conditions. Plants appear to wage successful war more easily than animals. The introduction of the Cactus in some parts of Cape Colony has locally modified both the fauna and flora, just as the Anacharis introduced into England spread from Cambridge over the whole country, and became for many years the predominant form of plant life in the streams. The Rabbit in Australia is a historic pest. Something similar to this physical fertility and increase appears to take place under new circumstances in certain organs within the bodies of animals, by the development of structures previously unknown. A familiar example is seen in the internal anatomy of the Trout introduced into New Zealand, where the number of pyloric appendages about the stomach has become rapidly augmented, while the size and the form of the animal have changed. The rapidity with which some of these changes have been brought about would appear to show that Nature is capable of transforming animals more rapidly than might have been inferred from their uniform life under ordinary circumstances. Growth of the vital organs in this way may modify the distinctive form of any vital organ, brain or lungs, and thus as a consequence of modification of the internal structures due to changes of food and habit, bring a new group of animals into existence. And just as the group of animals ceases to predominate after a time, so there comes a limit to the continued internal development of vital structures as their energy fails, for each organ behaves to some extent like an independent organism.

Under such explanations of the mutual relations of the parts of animals, and groups of animals, time ceases to be a factor of primary importance in their construction or elaboration. The supposed necessity for practically unlimited time to produce changes in the vital organs which separate animals into great orders or classes is a nightmare, born of hypothesis, and may be profitably dismissed. The geological evidence is too imperfect for dogmatism on speculative questions; but the nature of the affinities of Ornithosaurs to other animals has been established on a basis of comparison which has no need of theory to justify the facts. It is not improbable that the primary epoch of time, even as known at present, may be sufficiently long to contain the parent races from which Ornithosaurs and all their allies have arisen.

In thus stating the relation of Ornithosaurs to other animals the Flying Reptile has been traced home to kindred, though not to its actual parents or birthplace. There is no geological history of the rapid or gradual development of the wing finger, and although the wing membrane may be accepted as its cause of existence, the wing finger is powerfully developed in the oldest known Pterodactyles as in their latest representatives.

Pterodactyles show singularly little variation in structure in their geological history. We chronicle the loss of the tail and loss of teeth. There is also the loss of the outermost wing digit from the hind foot as a supporter of the wing membrane. But the other variations are in the length of the metacarpus, or of the neck, or head. One of the fundamental laws of life necessitates that when an animal type ceases to adapt its organisation and modify its structures to suit the altered circumstances forced upon it by revolutions of the earth's surface its life's history becomes broken. It must bend or break.

The final disappearance of these animals from the earth's history in the

Chalk may yet be modified by future discoveries, but the Flying Reptiles have vanished, in the same way as so many other groups of animals which were contemporary with them in the Secondary period of time. Such extinctions have been attributed to catastrophes, like the submergence of land, so that the habitations of animals became an area gradually decreasing in size, which at last disappeared. It appears also to be a law of life, illustrated by many extinct groups of animals, that they endure for geological ages, and having fought their battle in life's history, grow old and unable to continue the fight, and then disappear from the earth, giving place to more vigorous types adapted to live under new conditions.

The extinct Pterodactyles hold a relation to Birds in the scheme of life not unlike that which Monotremata hold to other Mammals. Both are remarkable for the variety of their affinities and resemblances to Reptiles. The Ornithosauria have long passed away; the Monotremes are nearing extinction. Both appear to be supplanted by parallel groups which were their contemporaries. Birds now fill the earth in a way that Flying Reptiles never surpassed; but their flight is made in a different manner, and the wing is extended to support the animal in the air, chiefly by appendages to the skin.

If these fossils have taught that Ornithosaurs have a community of soft vital organs with Dinosaurs and Birds, they have also gone some way towards proving that causes similar to those which determined the structural peculiarities of their bony framework, originated the special forms of respiratory organs and brain which lifted them out of association with existing Reptiles.

These old flying animals sleep through geological ages, not without honour, for the study of their story has illuminated the mode of origin of animals which survive them, and in cleaving the rocks to display their bones we have opened a new page of the book of life.

###